MEN OF OLD GREECE

RUINS OF THE PARTHENON

MEN OF OLD GREECE

BY

JENNIE HALL

YESTERDAY'S CLASSICS

CHAPEL HILL, NORTH CAROLINA

This edition, first published in 2008 by Yesterday's Classics, an imprint of Yesterday's Classics, LLC, is an unabridged republication of the work originally published by Little, Brown, and Company in 1905. For the complete listing of the books that are published by Yesterday's Classics, please visit www.yesterdaysclassics.com. Yesterday's Classics is the publishing arm of the Baldwin Online Children's Literature Project which presents the complete text of hundreds of classic books for children at www.mainlesson.com.

ISBN-10: 1-59915-270-3

ISBN-13: 978-1-59915-270-7

Yesterday's Classics, LLC
PO Box 3418
Chapel Hill, NC 27515

CONTENTS

PRONUNCIATION OF GREEK WORDS

Achilles (a kil′ ēz)
A crŏp′ o lis
Aegina (ē jī′ na)
Aesculapius
(es cu lā′ pi us)
Ag a mem′ non
Alcamenes (al cam′ e nēz)
Al cā′ nor
Alcestor (al kĕs′ tor)
Alcibiades (ăl sĭ bī′ a deez)
Alc mē′ nor
An ax an′ der
A pol′ lo
Ares (ā′ rēz)
Ar′ gŏs
Aristides (ăr is tī′ deez)
A ris′ ton
Ar′ te mis
A thē′ nē
At′ tĭ ca
Au′ go
Cer a mī′ cus
Cē phis′ sus
Chaerophon
(ker′ ĕ fon)
Charlicles (kar′ ĭ kleez)
chiton (kī′ tŏn)
chlamys (klă′ mis)
Cle om′ bro tus
Cle′ on
Cor′ inth
Crē′ on
Crī′ to
Delphi (dĕl′ fī)
Dem′ ĭ pho
Dī o ny′ sus
Erechtheum
(er ek the′ um)
Euboea (ū bē′ a)
Eu rō′ tas
Gy lip′ pus
hel′ ot
Hephaestus (he fĕs′ tus)
Heracles (her′ a klēz)

He′ re
Hermes (hẽr′ mēz)
Hetoemocles
(hĕ tem′ o kleez)
himation (hī mā′ shun)
Hip′ pi as
Hy met′ tus
Ic tī′ nus
I′ on
I′ rĕn
I′ ris
Lacedaemon
(las e dē′ mon)
Le on′ ĭ das
Lichas (lī′ kas)
Ly cur′ gus
Ly san′ der
Măr′ a thŏn
Me gis′ ti as
Mē′ no
met′ ō pē
Miltiades (mil tī′ a deez)
Odysseus (o dis′ soos)
O lym′ pĭ a
O lym′ pus
Pan ath ĕ nā′ ic
Pau sā′ nĭ as
Pē nel′ ō pē
Pen tĕl′ i cus
Pericles (per′ ĭ kleez)
Pheido (phī′ do)
Phidias (fĭd′ ĭ as)
Pheidippides
(phī dip′ pi deez)
Phō′ nax
Piraeus (pī rē′ us)
Pi san′ der
Plataea (pla tē′ a)
Pnyx (nĭks)
Poseidon (po sī′ don)
Săl′ a mis
Socrates (sŏk′ ra teez)
Soph ro nis′ cus
Taÿgetus (tā ij′ e tus)
Thebes (thēbz)
Themistocles
(the mĭs′ to kleez)
Thermopylae
(ther mop′ ĭ lē)
Theseus (thē soos)
Thespiae (thĕs′ pĭ ē)
Troezen (trē′ zen)
Xerxes (zerks′ eez)
Zē′ no
Zeus (zoos)

FOREWORD

THAT old Greece was a lovely land. Everywhere lines of peaked mountains looked at each other across pretty little valleys. Through the valleys sparkled small rivers. Beside the rivers stretched green olive groves, golden wheat fields, and garden-spots. Here and there, among the fields, shone white cities, with high walls and twisting streets. From the mountain-foot down to the flat valley lay hills, great and small. Their sides were streaked with vineyards and dotted with whitewashed cabins. On the mountain-side strayed sheep, watched by their shepherd, who was piping to himself in a cool cave. Every mountain-top looked off to the purple sea near at hand. This sea was dotted with ships and with rocky islands.

Up and down these islands and valleys and hillsides walked the beautiful Greeks. What made them beautiful? Their smooth skin, well rubbed with olive oil; their muscles, trained in the gymnasium; their shining eyes, happy with looking upon sea and mountain and statue and temple; and their clothes helped, too, for these were of bright colors and hung in gently moving folds. The busy vine-grower among his grapes, the shepherd walking the rough mountain, the sailor on his ship, the carpenter in his shop, wore short chitons, that left arms and legs bare and free. In the cool evening they clasped short capes about their shoulders. In the hot sun they tied broad hats on their heads. For a walk on a stony road they tied open sandals under their feet. The idle gentlemen of the cities threw about themselves himations,—great shawls, of thin wool or linen, that fell in soft folds from neck to feet. The women wore long, loose robes of the same sort.

Above this lovely land, and caring for it, were the gods. They lived in Olympus, a shining city among the stars. A golden wall, with clanging gates, went around it. Inside were sloping green meadows, sprinkled with wonderful flowers. Sitting among the flowers and grass were houses of gold and silver, the homes of the gods. On a little hilltop was a golden throne. Here sat Zeus, the king of the gods, the lord of the world. By his side sat Here, his queen. Around him stood the company of the gods, looking down upon the world.

There was Apollo, the beautiful, who by day drove the chariot of the sun across the sky. At night he sat here in Olympus, at the feast of the gods. He played on his lyre and sang such songs as common men have never heard. And there was Athene, in her armor of bronze. She took care of all the battles of the world, and she taught women to weave and men to work with tools. And there was Poseidon, who sometimes lived in a cave at the bottom of the sea. He made storms on the sea, and he calmed them. There was Hermes, who sent gentle winds to carry ships to the right port, and who flew through the air with the messages of Zeus. There was the boy-god, Dionysus, who sent dew and warmth to ripen the grapes of all the world. And there was Artemis, who drove the silver chariot of the moon and sometimes hunted the deer in the wildwood. There was the blacksmith god, Hephæstus. He could make statues of gold, that moved and walked about. There was Ares, the fierce god of war. And there was Demeter, who ripened the grain all over the world.

All these gods were like men and women, but taller, more beautiful and more wonderful. They could never die. Their eyes looked to the farthest edges of the world. No man could hide from them. They walked through the sky as quickly as thought. In the wink of an eye they could change from a god to a ragged shepherd lad or an eagle. Life was very gay and easy for them. And yet they had work to do. If Apollo had idled away a month in Olympus, the trees and plants and men down in the world would have died in the darkness. If Here had forgotten to visit the earth, no little babies would have come to happy mothers and fathers. If Dionysus had neglected his work, the grapevines and the pomegranate trees and the melon-vines all over the world would have died, and men would have been hungry for fruit, and thirsty for wine. If Poseidon had been angry and left the sea to storm, thousands of ships would have been wrecked, and sailors drowned. So the gods were a company of busy people, flitting about from city to city, from field to field, from sea to sea, and back to Olympus, to rest and feast and play. But they took care that men should not see them on those visits.

Now the Greeks down in the world loved these gods for their kindness. They wished to thank them. They wished to make them gifts. But they could not think how to do it; for they never saw the gods during their visits to the earth. Neither did they know what to send.

"The gods do not eat common food," they said, "but the sweet odors of the world are pleasant to them. Would they not like a taste of this meat and these fruits that they have given us? How shall we send them so far?"

Then they saw the smoke rising above the fire, above the house-top, above the trees, up into the sky.

"That is the way," they said.

So they built fires on little piles of sod. They soaked the sod with sweet-smelling wine. They put meat and fruits into the fires. The smoke caught the odors of wine, of crisping meat, and of toasting fruits, and whirled them up through the sky to Olympus. There the gods breathed the perfume and smiled down upon the blazing altars and the lifted hands.

Sometimes people built marble houses, or temples, around these altars. Here the gods might come to rest from their work in the world. Here people might come to bring gifts to the gods.

In such a land, among such people, under the eyes of these gods, lived the men of this book.

LEONIDAS

It was in one of the soldiers' huts at Sparta. Fifteen men, young and old, sat at mess. The heavy table before them had no cloth and few dishes. The seats were backless benches. The ceiling and walls of the hut were of rough, round logs. The floor was of dirt. Against one of the walls leaned long spears. The men were clothed in coarse gray chitons. There was no shine of gold or flash of color to make the place beautiful. But there were some things there more beautiful than gold or gay cloaks,—the men's broad shoulders, the working muscles of their brown arms, their high-lifted heads and tumbled hair.

While the others were eating, an old man spoke.

"I heard to-day of a good deed," he said. "It was of young Lysander there, our messmate."

As all eyes turned upon Lysander, he flushed and looked hard into his red bowl of broth.

"Three nights ago he went hunting on Mount Taÿgetus," the old man went on. "During the night Cleombrotus happened to pass by a deep rock-pit. He saw something move down there, and he called out

'Hello!' Nobody answered. He peered down and saw that it was a man in the pit. 'A bad fall,' said Cleombrotus. 'I will let down my hunting net and pull you out.' The answer came: 'You waste time. Does it take two men to get one man out of a hole?' So Cleombrotus came away chuckling. He knew Lysander's voice. I do not know how the lad got out, but I do know that he did not come back until to-day, and I saw that the skin was torn from his knees and toes and palms."

GREEK COSTUME
The youth wears a short chiton under a chlamys or cloak; the man is wearing a himation

Another man struck his hand upon the table.

"Done like a soldier and a Spartan!" he cried.

Lysander glanced up at him shyly with happy eyes.

Four little boys sat wide-eyed among these soldiers. The old man looked at the smallest one.

"What do you think of Lysander's deed, Leonidas?" he asked.

The boy drew in his breath quickly.

"I wish I had done it," he said.

The man sitting next the boy clapped him on the shoulder.

"So this is your first day away from home?" he laughed.

"Yes," answered Leonidas.

"Well, what do you think of our mess?"

"It is like being a soldier. I like it."

"Do you know why you came here ?"

"Because Sparta sent me."

"But why did Sparta send you?"

"She needs soldiers."

"Yes," the old man said with flashing eyes; "and we all are born only to be her soldiers. Is there a finer thing in the world than to fight for Sparta?"

"Did you cry this morning when you left home, Leonidas?" another man asked teasingly.

"No. Why should I cry? I have come to be a soldier. Spartans do not cry."

"But you did not like to leave your mother?"

"Sparta is my mother. And Sparta lives in the soldiers' huts. I have come to live with her. That is what my mother told me."

A man reached his hand across the table and said, smiling:

"Give me your hand, lad. Well said! But your manners need mending. Your mother has spoiled you. Boys should listen, not talk. A boy's great virtue is modesty."

The men rose from the table. It was night. They took their spears from the wall and walked away home. The lanes were dark and narrow, but the men carried no torches; for the Spartans had long ago made this law: "Men shall always walk in the city without torches, for in war they must march and scout in the dark."

The boys were still in the hut. One of the men, too, had stayed. It was his duty to look after the boys of Sparta. Now he called these lads to him and said:

"Remember Lichas' words: 'A boy's great virtue is modesty.' When you are with older men, your tongue cannot teach them, so let your ears learn. For that purpose you visit the men's mess. There you will hear more wisdom in one breath than you can speak in a whole day. Now report to your Iren. Remember—modesty! Your eyes on the ground! The gods give you sweet rest!"

The boys walked away slowly, their lips closed, their eyes turned to the ground. They went to another hut. It had but one large room. Here sat a young man in a heavy oak chair. A burning pine-torch was thrust into the wall above his head. The smoky light flickered dimly on perhaps twenty boys standing about. They were from seven to eighteen years old. A grown man leaned against the doorcasing, spear in hand. As the four boys came in, they walked up to the young man in the chair and gave their names, and said:

"Returned from Lichas' mess, Iren."

Iren was a name that meant captain of a boy's company.

"We are all in now," said the Iren. "Give us a song, Anaxander."

Anaxander took a lyre down from its peg on the wall. He ran his fingers over the strings and sang this song:

"I hope to fall in battle, sword in hand,
For men will sing and women praise me then.
'Here lies a Spartan hero dead,' they'll say;
'Let Sparta build for him a splendid tomb.
And on the tomb his statue high shall stand.
And Sparta's men and lads shall come to see
How well our Sparta loves the strong and brave.'

"Then raise the battle cry and draw your swords,
Press close together, comrades, into line.
Now sword and spear and death for Sparta's sake!

"But all men hate the coward that turns and flees;
From that most shameful day he longs for death,
For boys and women point at him and sneer,
And men all turn their heads aside and scowl.
He slinks from door to door to beg his bread,

He dares not show his face in Sparta's streets.
At last he dies of shame and finds no grave.

"Then raise the battle-cry and draw your swords,
Press close together, comrades, into line.
Now sword and spear and death for Sparta's sake!"

"Sparta, Sparta! A soldier's death for me!" shouted all the lads.

"A good song," said the Iren. "You shall teach our new boy, Leonidas, to sing and to play the lyre. To-morrow night I will see whether he has learned his strings. Leonidas, it is as much the duty of a soldier to sing as it is to fight. For how can he pray to the gods if he cannot sing? That puts courage into men's hearts."

Then he turned to another boy.

"Alcanor, what is the best thing in Sparta?"

The boy thought for a moment, and then answered:

"A hero's tomb. For it has in it a man who was brave, and it teaches other men to be brave."

"Well answered," said the Iren. "Pausanias, what makes a man brave?"

"Love of Sparta makes men brave," cried Pausanias.

"A bad answer!" said the Iren. "It is the laws of Sparta that make men brave. For do not the laws say that boys shall not live at home among the women, but in camp with soldiers? Do the laws not say that men shall walk without torches through the dark? Do the laws not say that cowards shall be punished? And is this not what makes our men brave? Come here. You shall be punished for your bad answer. Let this help you to remember what makes men brave."

As he said that he bit Pausanias' thumb. The thumb turned white under the teeth, but the boy did not wince. Then the Iren turned to some one else.

"Zeno, why should you steal flour for our bread to-morrow?"

"Because I am to be one of Sparta's soldiers," Zeno answered. "And when our army is in the enemy's country, there is no other way to get food."

"Good," said the Iren. "Go and do it. But if you are caught, you shall be punished. And if you get no flour, you shall not eat to-morrow."

As Zeno went out of the door, the Iren said to the others:

"Off to the Eurotas! If you do not want to sleep on the bare floor to-night, come back with your arms full of rushes. And be sure that you use no knife to cut them. A soldier's hands must take a few scratches."

So the boys scampered off through the dark to the river. Only the Iren and the man were left in the hut.

"Well done," said the man. "But in one thing you made a mistake. Pausanias' answer was a good one. The love of Sparta does make men brave. Often in a battle have I thought: 'Sparta is my mother.' Then my arm has grown strong, and my heart bold. Your answer, also, was true. But Sparta needs thoughtful officers. Let this remind you to think twice before you punish a boy again."

He struck the Iren across the legs with a leather strap.

"I will try to remember," the young man answered.

The other nodded and put his hand on the Iren's shoulder.

"The gods send sweet sleep to you!" he said. Then he walked away.

Soon the boys came straggling back. They threw their rushes down in a corner or next to the wall of the hut. Then, without undressing, they lay down upon them to sleep. There was nothing but the damp rushes to throw over themselves, if they grew cold. But every boy was proud of that, thinking,

"A soldier has nothing to cover him."

Leonidas came in among the last. His hands were cut and bleeding, but he thought, "I have to do this to be a soldier."

This thought made him happy.

At last everybody in the hut was asleep. And in other cabins all about, people were sleeping. Some camp-fires burned. Guards in armor, with spears in their hands, walked up and down. It was like a great camp in time of war. Yet there was no war and no fear of it. The men of Sparta always lived like this. They were always soldiers.

The next morning the boys were called at daybreak. There was no dressing, for they had slept in their clothes. There was only a run to the river and a cold plunge and a rough combing of hair with fingers. Then they ran back to the camp-ground. The older men were gathering there, every one with his spear. Many slaves were working about, building fires.

The different Irens called their boys together. Twenty or thirty companies stood in soldiers' order.

"Line up for the foot-race," called the Iren of Leonidas' group.

After the running, the Iren called to one of the larger boys:

"Come teach these little boys to box."

All over the field other companies were doing the same thing. The men walked among them, looking on. They gave praise when a boy did well. They stopped the game when it was wrong, and showed the right way to do. It was a busy, noisy, happy place.

After the boys had played for some time, a trumpet blew. Like a flash, all the men fell into line, bodies straight, heads up. Every man wore a red chiton that came to his knees. His feet and legs were bare. On his head shone a tall, egg-shaped helmet of bronze. A long shield hung on his left arm. On it was painted a great letter Λ. It stood for "Lacedæmon," the country of Sparta. At every man's left side hung his short broadsword. In his right hand he carried two or three lances. Their points glittered above his head.

By the side of the long line of men stood the officers. They passed down the order to march. Next came a quick command to swing into fours.

"That," said a boy to Leonidas, "is the way they march off to war."

Then the officers called out:

"Battle order, march!"

The eight fours at the head of the line stood still. The others marched up to the side of these, and stood. There were all the fighting men of Sparta, in deep, close line, ready to meet a foe.

"Sparta, Sparta!" shouted the boys who were watching.

The men drilled for an hour or more. Then the trumpet blew again, and they all walked away to their huts for breakfast. The slaves had it ready on the tables. It was not a rich meal. At every man's place was a red bowl of black broth. In the middle of the table were two large baskets of hard bread, a basket of fresh figs, and cheese on a wooden plate. There was no talking at first, for the men were hungry; but later it began. At Leonidas' table the old man who had told about Lysander spoke:

"Do you know why it is, boys, that we Spartans drill like this every day?"

"Because Spartans love to be soldiers," answered one of the lads.

"So we do," said the old man; and his eyes glowed. "But there is another reason, too. Hundreds of years ago the foster-father of Heracles was king in this southern country. But his enemy drove him out, and he fled north. Now Heracles' sons and his sons' sons never forgot that long ago one of their family had been king in this southern country. After a long time they said, 'We will go back to our old home.' So great hosts of them came, some by land, some by sea. This country was already full of people, living on farms and in cities. But the children of Heracles were mighty men, taller, stronger and braver than these people. So they fought with these men and won and made them slaves.

HERACLES

"The brave children of Heracles took the land and sat on the throne. These Helots who cook our breakfast and plow our fields and grind our flour and tend our cattle and make our wine and build our houses, are the far-off sons of the people who fought with those children of Heracles. Those men who live on the mountains and herd our sheep and work in our mines and smelt our iron and make our swords and cut our timber, are the children of the men who ran away. And we Spartans are the sons of those mighty children of Heracles. We are the lords of this land, the masters of these Helots.

"The Helots do not forget their free days. They hate us. They would be glad to drive us out. They are many more than we are. That is why a Spartan never walks without his spear. That is why we drill every day. That is why Sparta is a great camp. That is why we work to make ourselves good soldiers. A soldier must have strong muscles; so we exercise in hard games. A soldier must not be fat; so we eat little. A soldier must have time to drill; so we leave our work to the Helots. They are good laws that make us do these things. I think that Heracles must be proud as he looks down on us, his children, strong and brave."

During that afternoon the Iren of Leonidas' company called his boys together, and said:

"To-morrow we struggle at the Plane-tree Grove. Let us go now to ask Achilles for help. Bring gifts for him."

ACHILLES IN BATTLE

The boys ran to their hut. There seemed little there for gifts. But some brought pieces of hard bread saved from their breakfast.

"It is joy to go hungry and give to Achilles," one said.

Another brought a hunting spear.

"Achilles will like the smell of blood on this," he said.

One boy brought a wolf's head.

"Ah!" cried the Iren; "there is a gift that will please Achilles."

One was carrying a piece of iron as big as his hand.

"I suppose Achilles does not care for money," said he; "but this has a good name on it—Lacedæmon."

The Iren led a lamb.

They started across the country. The boy who had the piece of money told a story.

"I saw an Athenian in the market-place yesterday. He was as gay as a peacock. His hair was oiled and perfumed. He had a gold grasshopper pinned in it. His himation had a gold border. He had sandals on his feet. As though they were too good to touch the ground! Bah! He carried a little leather bag in his hand. I saw our good Ion looking at him and curling his lip. At last he said: 'Athenian, what is that you carry with so tender a hand?' 'My money-bag,' answered the stranger. He opened it and took out a little piece of gold and held it up. 'Is it not beautiful?' he said. 'There is nothing in all Sparta that shines like that. It would buy this whole poor city.' Ion looked at the man's foolish clothes, and smiled. 'No,' he said; 'its

AN ATHENIAN COIN

owner would never spend it for anything so well worth having.' Then he turned and walked away. I went with him. 'Do you see, Hippias,' he said to me, 'why we do not have gold money in Sparta? Can you imagine a man's carrying our iron money about and petting it? Surely our Lycurgus was wise. He saved us from being fools.' "

"There was only one Lycurgus," said the Iren; "that is why there is only one Sparta."

Soon the boys came to the temple of Achilles. A jar of salt water stood at the door. As the boys passed it, they dipped their hands into it.

"We must go into the houses of gods and heroes with clean hands," men said in those days.

Inside the door stood the priest in long white robes. A garland of flowers was on his head. The Iren said to him:

"We wish to get Achilles' help in our struggle to-morrow. We have brought this lamb to his table. We have other gifts for him."

"Achilles, the warrior, is glad to receive brave lads of Sparta in his house," said the priest.

He led the way to the altar. The boys laid their gifts upon it. The priest raised his hands and sang in a clear voice:

"Achilles, mighty warrior, brave and strong,
Oh! hear us in your happy island home;
Oh! smile on us and give us what we ask—
To win the game and make our Sparta proud."

Then flutes played shrill music. The priest killed the lamb and laid pieces of the meat on the altar-fire. Other pieces slaves cooked at another fire. They spread a table. All the boys sat down and ate with the priest.

"Achilles is our guest," the Iren said. "See the smoke curling up to him from the altar! It is a great thing to feast with such a man.

After the meal the boys walked back to Sparta. On the way they talked of the struggle to-morrow.

"We prove to-morrow whether we are good sons of Sparta," said the Iren. "I pray not to see a look of shame on my father's face. If we lose to-morrow, you know what it will say for me, your Iren."

"Never fear," cried Anaxander. "There is not a coward among us. If we lose, we can die. That will take away the shame."

On the next day the boys went to the Plane-tree Grove. There were walks and race-courses and gymnasium buildings. The fine old trees cast a pleasant shade. The boys ran down the broad walks.

"The bridge of Heracles!" they shouted. "Heracles is ours."

A little round island was in the middle of the grove. A broad moat full of water went around it. A bridge crossed the moat at each side of the island. On one bridge stood a statue of Heracles; on the other stood a statue of Lycurgus, the law-giver, the father of Sparta. The boys of Leonidas' company ran to the bridge of Heracles, the other boys to the other bridge.

They had cast lots the night before to see where they should stand. Men came hurrying from temple and gymnasium and shaded walks. All the Spartans were there to see what lads were brave and who were well drilled. They crowded to the edge of the moat. Some went upon the bridges behind the boys.

RUNNING TRACK AND GYMNASIUM IN SPARTA

The Gymnasium is at the right, the Altar and Statue of Heracles at the left

At a signal the two companies ran together. They met in the middle of the island. Then began a pushing. The game was for one side to push the other side into the water. At first they formed in solid blocks and pushed all together. But neither block moved. So they stood straining. Then different boys began to strike out with their fists. Some butted with their heads. Others rammed with their shoulders. The crowd broke up into couples, pushing, boxing, wrestling, falling, jumping up.

All this time the men on the shores and bridges were calling out:

"The boys of Heracles! Well struck, Hippias! Lycurgus! The boys of Lycurgus! To the water!"

Two boys were struggling near the bridge. The boy of Heracles was getting the worse of it. At last he broke away and ran toward the bridge. Then all the men hooted at him:

"Coward! Shame, shame! You are no son of Sparta! Shame!"

They closed together and stopped him. A man pushed to the front. He caught the boy by the shoulders.

"You are mad!" he cried. "It is better to die than to be a coward. I should be proud to carry you from here to your grave. But no coward shall ever call me father. Back, Damon, and show whose blood is in your veins." And he pushed him toward the island.

The boy looked at his father for a minute. Then his white face flushed red; He clenched his teeth and turned and ran at his opponent. He caught him around the waist and threw him. Then he dragged him along the ground toward the moat. But the other boy twisted and struck out at every step. So sometimes one was down, and sometimes the other. Sometimes both were rolling on the ground. Their arms were bruised, their legs were scratched. But at last Damon picked the boy up on his hip and swung him and threw him into the water. Then all those men on the bridges gave a great shout.

"Good, good, Damon! Sparta is proud of you." And they clapped the boy's father on the shoulder.

Damon had got his courage now. He did not stop. He ran to two other struggling boys and lent a hand.

THE WRESTLERS

The same things were happening all over the island. Boys were scattered about by twos or threes, pushing, dragging, wrestling. Now and then was a splash, when some one went into the water. Then all that was left for that one to do was to swim across and stand dripping on the other shore, watching his friends. One by one they were pushed in; sometimes a boy of Lycurgus, sometimes of Heracles, but most often of Lycurgus. At last only five boys were left on the island. Four of them were of Heracles. Then the four gave a shout and ran at the one and pushed him in and ran to the bridge, shouting:

"Victory, victory!"

"Heracles! The boys of Heracles!" shouted the men.

They ran to meet the four boys. They lifted them upon their shields and went shouting up and down the walks.

"The heroes of Sparta," they cried.

The other boys of their company went dancing around them.

"Our heroes," they shouted; "the favorites of Achilles! He is our friend. Smile down, O Heracles!"

Lysander was one who was carried high on a shield. His face was pale. His lips were shut hard. His left arm hung broken. But his eyes were wide and shining with joy. What of his broken arm! Sparta was proud of him.

Damon, who at first had tried to run away, was another who was carried on a shield. His father walked behind him. He looked proudly at his son.

Leonidas had been pushed into the water. He was only seven years old, and it was his first game. But he had not been afraid. He had done his best. Now Ion came to him.

"You did well, lad," he said.

He held out his hand, and Leonidas took it.

"Come with me," the old man said. "Let us walk about the city. There are many things to see."

Leonidas looked up proudly at Ion. It was good to hold that old man's hand. It was good to get his smile. He was a senator,—a great man and a wise one. He gave advice to the kings. Here he was talking to a little boy. He was saying:

"You have done such good work to-day that I want to show you the statue of a man who did still better things in a game. It is pleasant to an old man to see lads brave and quick and strong, with straight, tough bodies. Years ago my own boy won at the Plane-tree Grove. I was more proud then than I should have been to see him king. Some of us never can be kings, but we can be soldiers. But your grandfather was a king. We expect great things of you."

The streets they were walking down were strange looking. They were like country lanes. A footpath wound through the grass. On either side were houses. They were made of squared logs, unpainted, and brown with age. The rough marks of the axe showed. The roof was flat and low. One wide door opened in the front. Around every house were wheat fields and gardens, with grapevines, olive trees, pomegranate trees, bee-hives. Slaves were working there.

"I myself have never been out of Sparta," Ion said, "and I am glad of it. But I once talked with a man from Athens. That is a city north of us. From what he said I thought Athens must be a poor place. To begin with, they have a high wall around their city. As though the people were pigs, to be fenced in! And besides, it shows that they are afraid, to protect themselves with a wall. Our good swords and right arms are our wall. No enemy can break through them. Inside of their little walls the Athenians crowd all their people. That leaves no room for gardens. I do not see how those men can breathe. See our green fields and trees! See the good breeze of Zeus playing in them! We have room to stretch ourselves, and air to breathe. O Sparta, Sparta, beautiful strong mother!"

Leonidas looked up shyly and blushed.

"I shall fight for her some time," he said. "Perhaps I shall die for her."

"There is no greater good fortune," Ion answered.

He stopped now before a statue. It was of a man. His right foot was pushed before him. He was bent forward. He was reaching out with his arms. A fierce frown was on his brow. The muscles stood out on his slender bare body.

"Oh!" cried Leonidas; "he would win at the Plane-tree Grove."

"That," Ion said, "is Hetœmocles. For twenty years he was the best wrestler in Greece, and that means in the world. Five different times he went across the mountains to the great games at Olympia. The best men from all the cities of Greece were there. They wrestled with him, but he never lost. From every game he brought home an olive crown. The people of Sparta had this statue made in his honor. It is such men as this that make Sparta famous and strong. You began well to-day. Perhaps I shall live to see your statue beside his."

A mist came into Leonidas' eyes when he heard that. The blood rushed into his face.

"I cannot hope for that," he said, "but I will try not to make Sparta ashamed."

They walked on down the street. Farther on the houses were close together. There were statues between them instead of gardens,—Apollo here, Zeus there, farther on Dionysus, across the street a victor of Olympia, some old king, a great battle hero. Ion had something to say of every one as they passed.

"It is good for you to come often and see these gods and these great men," he said. "You must not make them ashamed. Great men have walked this ground and loved it. Long ago Menelaus was our king. His house still stands over yonder. He and the beautiful Helen lie buried across the Eurotas. Odysseus came here to get Penelope. Not far off the Great Agamemnon lies in his tomb. There is not one of the gods that has not put foot in Sparta. It is holy ground. Let not your foot make it unholy."

It was a busy life for Leonidas now. Every night he must pull rushes for his bed. Every morning he must drill with the company. For long hours every day he must go to the gymnasium in the Plane-tree Grove. Ion was often there to watch him. After work was finished the old man took the boy for a walk. Sometimes it was along the banks of the Eurotas, out into the country. Sometimes it was about the city, to see the statues and public buildings.

Always Leonidas learned something new during those walks. Perhaps Ion told him the story of Troy or of some god. Perhaps he taught him some wise saying of Lycurgus. Perhaps he took stones and showed him how to count. Perhaps, as they stood before a statue, Leonidas learned to spell out the name of Zeus or of Heracles or of Sparta. Perhaps Ion taught him to sing a battle-song. Leonidas had no other school than these tales and the gymnasium.

That gymnasium was to Leonidas the pleasantest place in Sparta. At the entrance stood a bronze statue of Heracles. Porches ran around the four sides of a court. Back of them opened the wide doors of dressing-rooms. Men were walking along the porches, talking and laughing. Ion leaned against one of the columns. The court was filled with boys at work. Some were throwing the disc. This was a round plate of lead or of stone. It was thick in the middle and thinner at the edges. The thrower held it in his right hand. He swung it back and forth, to get a good movement. Then he threw it. The game was to find who could throw the farthest.

Some boys were jumping. The jumper held a lead weight in each hand. He swung them back and forth, to give himself a good start. Then he threw them behind him and jumped. That backward push sent him ahead.

Other boys were throwing spears at a mark.

These spears had leather straps wound around them at the balancing point. The thrower put his finger through the loop. When he threw, he held the strap for a second. That made the spear whirl. It bored into the target.

With every group of boys was a teacher. He allowed no laziness.

"You are not here to play," he said. "You are here to get good bodies and to learn to be good soldiers. It is a hard task. Sparta is watching you."

INTERIOR OF THE GYMNASIUM

Leonidas, on his first day, went into a dressing-room and threw off his chiton. When he came out into the court, a teacher met him. He looked the boy over carefully.

"Go to the running-tracks," he said. "Your legs are too thin."

The running-track opened out of the court. It was a long, smooth path. At each end was a post. On top of the post stood a little statue of Victory. So Leonidas ran here and rested, and ran again and again. Then he went back to the shady porch to rest.

Some slaves sat in one corner playing on trumpets and drums. In the court boys were dancing to this war-music. They were pretending to be warriors. They carried shields and swords. They moved forward and struck out with their swords. Then they leaped to the side and put up their shields. They were pretending to catch a stroke from an enemy. Then they peered over their shields and struck out from under them. They ran forward and struck fast. They were chasing the enemy. All this they did in time to the music, yet it looked almost like a real battle. It was hard work. The boys' bodies were dripping. Their eyes and cheeks glowed. At the end they turned and came dancing gayly to the porch. They held their shields high over their heads. They waved their swords. They sang a song of victory. The people watching cheered and clapped their hands.

Then Leonidas went to Ion, ready to walk. His face was flushed from the hard work. His eyes were dancing. When Ion saw him, he said, smiling,

"Apollo of the track has breathed color and life into you, little runner."

"I can dance that dance," Leonidas said as they walked away. "My mother taught it to me when I was at home. I danced it with my sisters. My mother said to them: "We women shall never fight, but our sons will; so let us learn the dance. Sparta wants mothers who can take good care of their children; so let us run and wrestle and throw the disc and the spear, to make ourselves well and strong.' They used to go to a gymnasium where there were only girls."

SPARTAN GIRLS WITH CITHARA

"Yes," answered Ion; "and that is what makes our Spartan girls beautiful, and our Spartan mothers brave."

Leonidas was eighteen years old. He was walking with Ion on the river bank after mess. The dark was coming on.

"So to-morrow you become a man, my boy," Ion was saying; "a soldier of Sparta. We have been friends for a long time, Leonidas,—eleven years. I have seen you grow tall. I have seen your shoulders broaden. I have seen your muscles harden. I have seen the fire of courage lighted in your eyes. I have seen your heart grow big. I am an old man. I shall not do much more work for Sparta, but I am proud of this, my last piece of work, this boy that has grown up under my hand. Has it been a hard life, Leonidas?"

"Yes, hard," the boy answered, "but very sweet. I have been working for Sparta, and I love her."

"Yes, I can see love for Sparta shining in your face every day," Ion said. "You have never shrunk from pain and hard work. You have never complained. The hardest trial of all comes to-morrow. But I believe that you will go through it well. Some will fail and will be sent away from Sparta with fingers pointed at them. But you will not fail. And you will remember, too, that Sparta does it all in love. She will lash your back until the blood flows. But you will kneel at Heracles' altar and smile; for you will know that if you cannot bear pain, it is better that you go away now. If you stayed, you would some time shame yourself and your family and Sparta and Heracles in battle. You will get your sword to-morrow. Shall a man carry a sword if he is afraid of the cut of a whip? Your grandfather was a king of Sparta. Your brother is king now. But it is a poor thing to have men point at you and say: 'There is the brother of a king.' It is a fine thing to have them say of you: 'There goes a Spartan.'

"But no more talk now. It is time for you to report to the Iren."

On the next day things happened as Ion had said. Leonidas walked away from Heracles' altar with a bleeding back, but his heart sang for joy. He was a man! He had been found brave enough to save Sparta. Perhaps he would be chosen Iren of some boys' company. Before long he could be a captain of Helots. Soon he could join a mess. He thought of the mess he would like to join. It was the Iren's old company. But his friend was more than sixty years old now. So he lived at home and did no soldier's work.

"I will get them a boar for supper," Leonidas thought.

Off he ran to the west, towards Mount Taÿgetus. On the way he stopped at a little hut.

"Pisander!" he called.

A young man came out. He was a Helot. He was not so tall or so strong as Leonidas. His skin was not so smooth and clear. His hands were stiff from holding the spade. Yet he was a fine-looking lad.

"Come for a hunt," Leonidas said.

Pisander's face lighted up.

"Artemis give us luck!" he cried, and started off on a run beside Leonidas. "Hare or deer?" he asked.

"Boar," answered Leonidas.

Pisander stopped short. "You go to hunt boar with only two people?" he cried. "We shall be killed."

Leonidas had kept on running. He called back over his shoulder,

"Don't come if you are afraid."

"I'm not," shouted Pisander, and started on again.

"There are dogs at Ion's," Leonidas said.

Soon they stopped before a house. In the garden at the side were dog-kennels. The boys went there. They took down five leashes and collars from a peg in the fence. Inside were a dozen dogs barking and leaping up. Leonidas and Pisander went into the yard. They picked out five of the largest dogs and put the collars on them and led them out. Then they went to a little shed and opened it. There lay nets piled up. Spears of all kinds leaned against the walls.

"We will not take nets," said Leonidas; "this is to be a fair fight between the boar and me."

Each boy took three spears. One was long, with a slim, sharp tip. One was short, with a heavy shaft and broad point. One had long guards sticking out halfway up the shaft. These dogs and spears and nets belonged to the city. Any Spartan had a right to take them whenever he needed.

The two boys walked on toward the mountain. Their matted yellow hair shone in the sun. The wind waved their short gray chitons. The spears glistened above their heads. Their bare arms and legs flashed white over the green grass. The dogs barked and leaped about them and tugged at their leashes. Suddenly Leonidas stopped and lifted his hands to the sky.

ARTEMIS

"O Artemis, huntress, I vow to give you a share of our game. Give us good luck."

As he walked on, he said:

"It is a hot day. I think we can run him down easily."

Now they were making a steep climb. They were going through a forest. The dogs kept sniffing the ground. The boys looked to right and left for marks of a boar. They wound out of the forest and came upon a high cliff.

"Ah!" cried Leonidas, and pointed. "See! Sparta! The blue Eurotas and its flat, green valley! The market-place, with its crowd of buildings! The temples, scattered everywhere among the trees! North are the mountains that shut us out from our enemies. That is the country I would die for, Pisander." And he turned and walked on up the mountains.

Soon one of the dogs began to pull hard at the leash. She put her nose to the ground and wagged her tail.

"She has a track," whispered Leonidas.

"See!" cried Pisander, pointing to a tree. "The mark of a tusk on the bark."

Now another dog got the scent.

"Unleash Augo," said Leonidas.

Pisander did it, and the first dog ran ahead, with nose to the ground. But soon she stopped and ran about in one spot.

"She has lost it," said Leonidas.

He gave his dogs to Pisander to hold. Then he went to Augo.

"Well done, Augo," he said, "well done! Get it! Get it!"

He looked about for a tusk-mark or a footprint or a broken twig. He found nothing.

"Let go Phonax," he called to Pisander.

Then Phonax came running along the track. But she, too, lost the scent. At last Leonidas said:

"It is cold. Let us go."

They had that same luck all day long.

"No sleep or supper until we have a boar," said Leonidas.

So they kept on until it was dark. They could not see the ground well. Often they stepped on sharp stones and cut their feet. It was cold on the mountain.

"We must run, to keep from getting stiff," Leonidas said. "When the moon comes out, we may have better luck. May Artemis smile!"

Soon the moon rose. The sky was clear. The great mountain lighted up. Its white rocks gleamed. Little streams glistened. The light pushed among the trees and showed the bushes and paths. The boys stopped to drink at a spring.

"Look!" cried Leonidas. "The mark of a boar's foot in the mud! Augo, Phonax! Smell, smell!"

In a flash the dogs had the scent. Leonidas undid the leashes. Off they shot up the mountain, noses to the ground. The boys ran after, through forest, over rocks, across streams. They ran for miles. The dogs were far ahead.

"Did you hear?" Leonidas cried at last. "They are barking. They have him. Faster!"

Soon they came upon the dogs. They were in a circle about a clump of bushes. Every dog was looking into it and barking. The boys could see nothing, for the bushes were thick and close to the ground.

"Beat the bushes, Pisander," said Leonidas, "and I will stand ready."

So Pisander beat the bushes with his spear. There was a rustle, and the boar rushed out. He caught one of the dogs on his tusk and threw him into the air and against Leonidas. The boy stood on the edge of a small rock. This stroke pushed him off, and he fell. The boar ran past him down the mountain.

"I have lost him!" Leonidas cried. "Clumsy foot!"

He was up and after. The dogs ran ahead of him. After a long run, they were barking again. In a moment Leonidas was up with them. The boar was facing them. Behind him was a gorge. The wall of stone dropped straight down. The boar had run into a trap. He could not jump, so he had turned to fight the dogs. Leonidas came close, among the dogs, and thrust at him with his spear, but he only gave the shoulder a little cut. The boar dashed at him madly. Leonidas leaped away. Then he found that he had leaped to the wrong side. His back was to the gorge. He and the boar had changed places. The beast rushed at him again, but Leonidas stood ready and ran his broad spear through the neck. But the boar's rush pushed him back, and his feet slipped over the edge of the gorge. As he fell, he caught at a tree. There he hung by one arm. His head was only a little above the top of the ground. The boar was still able to fight; he was pushing at the spear, trying to reach Leonidas. His tusks were within a span of the boy's face, The shaft of the spear was slipping and bending.

"O Artemis, help me!" breathed Leonidas.

* * * * *

After a few minutes, Pisander ran up, puffing. He stopped short when he saw Leonidas. The Spartan was standing with hands raised to the bright moon.

"O Artemis," he was praying, "queen of the hunt, queen of the moon, Artemis, mountain-dweller, Artemis of the flying feet, of the moonlit eyes, Artemis, saver of life, your altar shall remember this night! The smoke of my sacrifice shall carry to you the heart of Leonidas and his thanks. Every morning I will send a prayer to you in Olympus, and every night in the moon."

"What is it?" asked Pisander.

"O Pisander, we are in the hands of the gods," Leonidas said. "Just now I hung over that gorge. By my left hand I held to a tree. Through my right my spear was slipping. The boar's breath was in my face. His tusks scratched my hand. He was pushing nearer. Then I called upon Artemis for help. The moon was under a cloud; but Artemis put aside the clouds, and with her beams she shot into my heart her own courage and into my limbs her own strength. She sent a strange voice into the woods. The boar stopped to listen. Then in that moment, with the strength that Artemis had given me, I pulled myself up to the ground, and lo! the boar was dead. Do not the feet of the gods make our land holy? They hide in our forests. They walk on the winds about us. They watch us from sun and moon. Their eyes are always upon us. Their hands are ever ready to help."

The boys stood silent for a little while. They were thinking of the wonderful gods. Then Pisander quietly began to leash the dogs. Leonidas tied the feet of the boar together and hung it over a pole. Each boy took an end over his shoulder, and they started down the mountain.

They reached Ion's house in the early morning. The light was just beginning to grow in the sky. They shut up the dogs and put away the spears. Leonidas took a hunting-knife and cut off a shoulder of the boar and gave it to Pisander.

"Here is your share," he said. "May the gods give you good appetite!"

Then he walked on to the training-grounds, the boar across his shoulders. Helots were building the fires. Leonidas went up to one of these groups and laid the boar on the ground.

"This is for your masters' mess," he said.

He cut off a hind quarter, saying:

"This much belongs to Artemis."

He walked through the city to an altar of Artemis. He laid the boar's flesh upon the fire. He kissed the statue that stood there. He raised his hands and sang a prayer. The rising sun shone in upon him, on his yellow hair, his fluttering chiton, his lifted hands.

THERMOPYLÆ

An army lay encamped on a little plain. At one side was the sea. On the other rose a steep mountain, with its oaks and pines. In front of the army the mountain came close to the water. An ox-cart could just go between sea and hill. Across this place was a stone-wall, with a gate. Behind the army was another narrow pass. The place was called the pass of Thermopylæ. North of it lay part of Greece. South of it lay the other part, where Athens and Sparta were. Between these parts were steep mountains. Thermopylæ was like a gate in that mountain-wall. It was the only good road from north to south. This army was here now to guard it.

The Persians from across the sea were marching down toward the south. This news flew ahead of them:

"The king himself is coming. His army drinks rivers dry. Whole cities grow poor in feeding it. It stretches, glittering like the sea. The Greeks bow down as the king comes near. He meets no foes. The land is afraid. He comes to make us slaves."

The men of Southern Greece said:

"We must stop those Persians. Thermopylæ is the place. We must send an army."

"There is no hurry," the Spartans said. "They are yet far off. It is time for the great festival at Olympia. We must stay for that. But we will send a few men as a promise. More will come later!"

So the Spartan king went with his guard of three hundred men. That little army was fine to look at as it swung out of the city in double line, with shining armor and red chitons and long bronze shields and tall bronze helmets and dangling swords and stiff lances. And the king who led this army was Leonidas; for his brother had died and had left no sons.

These soldiers marched their long way through the country. People came to look at them.

"Sparta surely makes warriors," they thought.

A few cities, seeing them, said,

"We will help."

So other soldiers joined Leonidas. From one city came eighty; from another, a thousand; from Thebes, four hundred; from Thespiæ, seven hundred. But, after all, it was only a little company.

Now this army was in camp at Thermopylæ. Tents were dotted over the little plain. Mules and horses were feeding in the grass. The rough carts were drawn into a circle. Some of the soldiers were at work. They were building up the old wall across the pass. Others were playing games,—running, throwing the disc, dancing, wrestling. The red chitons of the Spartans showed bright in the crowd. One of these Spartans was saying to a Theban:

"War is our play. You think it a hardship. You feast in time of peace. We feast in time of war. You put on gay clothes for a visit. We wear rags in peace, and fine things for war. You curl your hair for a banquet. We go cut and uncombed to table. Our hair grows long for war, and we dress it for battle; for lions must have manes."

"Have you seen the army of the Great King?" asked the other man, pointing past the mountains.

"Yes," answered the Spartan. "Yesterday I was a scout. An hour's walk from our camp lie the Persians. Their tents are as many as the stars. The foolish king has had a great throne put up. There he sits and looks about."

"I suppose he is waiting for us to run away," said the Theban.

"Perhaps," laughed the Spartan. "Have you heard of the man who sat down to see a river turn and run uphill?"

"Meanwhile," said the Theban, "we play our games and have our drills and sharpen our swords."

So the armies sat for four days. But on the fifth morning a Greek scout came running into camp.

"At last the fish bites!" he cried. "They are coming, but only one company of them."

Then there was a rushing to arms.

"You Spartans look as though the best course of the banquet were being served," said a Theban.

"So it is," shouted a dozen Spartans.

The men fell into line at Leonidas' command. The gates were opened, and they marched out. They formed in a deep mass before the wall. They waited. Soon there was a glint of bronze from around a hill. Then sounded horses' hoofs. Still the Greeks waited. Leonidas stood in front of his Spartans. He was tall and straight. His head was high. His blue eyes blazed. His brown arms, rough with big muscles, held ready shield and spears.

The hoof-beats and the shining armor came nearer. Now the Persians were in full view—thousands of men on running horses. Brilliant cloths fluttered from their heads. A strange iron dress, like the scales of a fish, shone on their bodies. Wide scarlet trousers flapped in the wind. Every man leaned forward as he rode. At last they pulled their long bows and let fly their arrows. They yelled strange words. They came on like a whirlwind. The Greeks waited until the Persians were crowded together in the narrow pass just in front of them. Then they opened their mouths and shouted their good war-cry and blew their shrill trumpets. They swung their swords and ran into that crowd of Persians. Then was the noise of a great fight,—clashing of swords, whizzing of arrows, shouting of men. From morning until afternoon they fought. Greeks fell dead under Persian arrows, but more Persians under Greek swords. At last the enemies' arrows were gone, their spears were broken. They were bleeding with wounds and stiff with fighting. And still the Greeks stood like a wall of biting swords. So at last the Persians turned in fear and rode back to their camp.

PERSIAN SOLDIERS

The Greeks sat down in front of the wall to rest. They sat as they were, in their armor, their spears in their hands. They knew that a million Persians waited back of the hills. They ate a quick meal. They carried their wounded behind the wall. The Spartans cleaned their armor and combed their long hair. But all the time the warriors kept their eyes on the pass ahead. At last they saw again the flash of bronze and heard the clatter of hoofs. In a moment the Greeks were on their feet and in line of battle. This time there swung into view ten thousand gay horsemen.

"They are the king's own guard," called out a Greek. "This is the flower of their army."

"The Great King flatters us," said a Spartan, smiling, as he felt the edge of his sword.

Again the Greeks and Persians met. The Greeks were tired from the other battle: the Persians were fresh. Yet the Greeks stood. But the Persians were doing brave deeds. Neither side could force the other back. They stood struggling for an hour. At length Leonidas gave a signal. Then his men turned their backs and all ran toward the wall. When the Persians saw them running away, they shouted and clapped their heels to their horses and rode after them. They laughed and waved their swords and forgot to be careful. That was what Leonidas wanted. At last he gave another signal, and the Greeks turned in a flash and marched back against the Persians and cut them down and made them flee to camp.

That was near night. Then the Greeks built fires before the walls and cooked their suppers and ate. Every man slept in his armor that night, with his spear by his hand.

All the next day there was fighting, but the Greeks stood their ground, and the Persians ran away.

Before supper that night, Leonidas said:

"Let us sacrifice to the gods for our good battle."

So they put meat and wine into the fire that burned on a sod altar. As the smoke went up, Leonidas raised his hands and cried:

"O great Zeus, and Ares, father of battles, and Athene of the bright shield, and all the gods who have fought with Greece to-day, receive our thanks!"

ARES DESCENDING TO BATTLE

Then all the soldiers standing about raised a great song of thanksgiving. After that, Leonidas said to a man near him:

"Megistias, you are wise in reading the signs of what will happen. Come and look at the sacrifice and tell us of to-morrow."

Then Megistias came and studied the fire. He noticed the color of the flame and the direction of the smoke and many other things. Then he stepped upon a pile of sod. There was no joy in his face. He raised his hands over the camp.

"O ye Spartans and other Greeks, the gods send you the good luck of dying in battle! To-morrow your wives will be widows, your sons orphans. We shall lie here dead, and the Persians will march past us to Greece."

Leonidas leaped upon the sod.

"Then they will meet our brothers, more brave and of better luck. It is no mean thing to die here for Sparta and for Greece. Let us make ready for a noble death that men shall talk about."

As the Spartans sat about the camp-fire after supper, one of them took his lyre in his hands and stood among his countrymen and sang:

"A foe, a sword,
Our land to guard,
The gods to watch,
A grave, a stone,
A song of praise—
Enough for me."

Then he gave the lyre to the man next him. This was his song:

"They say that some men sit and feast
And spend their nights in drink and song,
And idly sleep their days away.

Such men are laughter to the gods,
A shame unto themselves and Greece.
How do the Spartans spend their time?
In drills and games and mess and hunts,
To make them fit for death like this."

The singer passed on the lyre, and the next man sang:

"For what do we fight, O Spartan men?
O memories dear; O Spartan land;
O heroes of old, in Sparta dead;
O tombs of our kings, who Sparta loved;
Lycurgus the wise, the Spartan seer;
O shrines of the gods, who Sparta trod;
O mothers and wives in Sparta now.
For these things we die, O Spartan men."

So they passed an hour or more in song. Around the other camp-fires different things were happening. At some, men sat silent, with white faces. Around others were grumbling and angry looks.

"These Spartan fools!" some men said. "Hear them boast! They would fight against the sea itself."

Two or three hours after dark a guard came to Leonidas, leading a man.

"This man came running to me now," he said. "He calls himself a Greek, a deserter from the Great King."

The stranger turned to the men and spoke.

"I am a Greek from across the sea," he said. "You know how the Great King has crushed us with his heavy hands. After that he said, 'You shall go with me to fight against your countrymen!' —But I did not come to tell you my story, but this news: The Persian army is moving. They are crossing the mountains at your left. A traitor told them of the path. They broke camp at lamplighting time. Part stayed behind. In the morning they will close around you from front and back and wipe you out. I swear by the gods that I speak the truth!"

"We believe you," said Leonidas quietly. "A prophet has already told us that we shall die to-morrow."

Just then another deserter was brought in. He told the same story.

"We put some men to guard that path," Leonidas said; "but they are few. The path is little known. We thought the Great King would not hear of it. Besides, it is narrow and steep. So he would rather face the mountain than the Spartans?" he laughed. "But we need sleep to make us ready for the fight. The gods give us sweet rest, comrades!"

So the Spartans slept calmly all night.

Before sunrise next morning the Greeks were at breakfast. As they ate, scouts came running down the mountain-side. They leaped, panting, among the men.

"They are crossing the mountain. They will shut us in from behind and in front."

Then there was murmuring among the Greeks. Leonidas heard it and said:

"Come close, all you men of Greece. Let us talk

this matter over. It is my opinion that we ought to stay and fight. How many think with me?"

Every Spartan and Thespian hand shot up with a shout.

"It is folly," cried out a Theban. "Do you think you can stop a million men?"

"No," answered a Spartan. "Neither can we run away."

"Do you know how many there are?" called another man. "When they shoot their arrows, they will hide the sun."

"So much the better," laughed a Spartan. "We shall fight in the shade."

"Let the Spartans stay," called another Theban. "They are afraid to go back home. But we have mothers and wives who love us."

"And we Thespians will stay," shouted a man, "because we have mothers and wives whom we love."

At last Leonidas spoke.

"O men of Greece!" he said, "we Spartans were sent here to guard this pass. There is nothing else for us to do. But your commands are not so strong. You have different laws. It is needless for you to stay. It means only death. The Persians are still on the mountain. The way to the south is clear. I send you to your homes. The Thespians stay with us from choice. The Thebans stay because I command it. We have heard whispers of what they wish to do,—to join the Persians. To you others, farewell! May the gods keep you to fight against our enemies another day!"

Then Leonidas went to Megistias.

"No man will go alive from this field," he said. "You can give the messages of the gods to men. Go with these soldiers and save your life."

"No!" said Megistias, "I will not leave the company of the brave for the company of cowards."

So those others marched away south. Those who were left waited until about noon. They cleaned their armor and got their weapons ready and talked quietly of what was coming.

"Here are our graves," one said, looking about the little plain. "But, by Heracles! here are some Persian graves, too."

"We fight in the sight of our gods and by their holy altars," Leonidas said. "For see, yonder is a healing spring of Heracles, and his altar by it. I pray that we may not make him ashamed of his children."

At last there came the trampling of horses from the north. Then the Greeks marched out of the gate and on past the narrow place. They spread out into a thin line and went on to meet the Persians. Then the fight began. A god seemed to burn in every Greek. The Persians fell fast. Then they grew afraid and tried to turn back, but those behind pushed them ahead. And at the back the officers whipped their men into the fight. So some were trampled down, others were pushed into the sea. Soon all the Greek spears were broken or lost. The men fought only with their short swords. Then many of them died, and Leonidas was one. When he fell, the Persians gave a great shout and rushed to get his body. But the Greeks cried out, "Sparta and Leonidas!" and closed around him in a circle, with swords flashing death. So they stood for a long time fighting. But at last the word went about,

"The other Persians are coming from behind."

Then those Spartans and Thespians who were left took up Leonidas and carried him back to a little hill behind the wall, fighting all the way. But the Thebans ran to the Persians and held out their hands, crying,

"We are friends of the Great King."

So the Persians passed them by and went on to the hill. On the top was that little ring of brave men, facing out to their foes on every side. But such a thing could not last long. That sea of Persians swept up the hill and left every Spartan and Thespian dead and went on into Greece.

After that there was a terrible war. But when it was over, and the Persians were driven out, the Greeks said,

"Our children's children must know what happened at Thermopylæ."

So they raised a great mound over the dead there and set up two columns. One was for all who fought on those first two days. There were carved on it these words,

"Four thousand Greeks here fought against a million Persians."

The other column was for the Spartans alone. On it were these words,

"Stranger, go tell Sparta that we lie here at her command."

But on that little hill where the Spartans made their last stand was another monument, a stone lion, with "Leonidas" carved upon it.

MARKET-PLACE OF SPARTA
Persian Hall at the right; Citadel at the rear; Statue of the Spartan People in the centre

Sparta never forgot that battle or that hero. In her market-place she built a covered walk, called the Persian Walk. Instead of columns to hold up the roof, were Persians carved in stone, and on the wall of the porch were paintings of the Persian battles. That porch seemed always to say,

"Remember the courage of the men who drove the Persians out of Greece."

Four years after the battle of Thermopylæ, the Spartans said:

"Our greatest hero lies in strange soil. Let us bring him home. It will do our sons good always to see his tomb."

So they brought the bones of Leonidas to Sparta, and buried them in a great stone tomb. And there they hung a bronze tablet, with the names of those three hundred Spartans on it, and these words,

"These are the men who looked the Persians in the face."

Every year at this tomb there were games and speeches. Only Spartans might play, and only Spartans might hear.

"Other heroes sleep in Spartan soil," those speakers said. "Here sleeps the lion of Thermopylæ. He was a king. He was a Spartan. Let Spartans see that they be worthy of this countryman and of this king."

THEMISTOCLES

All the freemen of Athens stood on the Pnyx hill. There were tanners and carpenters and farmers and fishermen, in short, dark chitons. Their brown arms and legs were bare. Their hair was cropped. There were gentlemen in white linen robes that reached to their feet. Their long hair was gathered into a knot on top of their heads and was fastened with a golden pin. Here and there a few young men were dressed in a later fashion. Their hair was short. They wore short chitons, like the workmen's. But these glowed with gold embroidery or light bands of color.

There were no smiling faces in that great crowd. Most wore sneers or frowns. All eyes were turned toward the stone platform. There was a strange company. One man stepped out to speak. He wore a long red robe of silk, embroidered with flowers. On his head was a tall red cap. His black hair hung in curls to his shoulders. His face was dark and covered with a curling beard. A heavy gold chain hung around his neck. He raised his hand to speak, and a loose sleeve fluttered out. Gold bracelets shone on his arm. On the platform were two or three other men dressed in the same fashion. The Athenian officer, the president of the meeting, sat in a chair. His chin was in his hand. He looked at the stranger and frowned.

REMAINS OF THE PNYX

This stranger began to speak. But he used a language that the Athenians could not understand. A man stood beside him. He had fair face and hair like the Athenians, and he wore a long chiton like theirs. He was a Greek from across the sea, where these strangers lived, and he could speak their language. He had come with them to tell the Athenians what they said. So now, as the stranger talked, this Greek spoke after him:

"I am a messenger to you from the Great King of Persia. He is master of the world, The harvests of the great Nile are his. The ships on the paths of the sea are his. The horses of Arabia, the gold of India, belong to him. The wild men of the north bow down to him. Lands tremble under the glance of his eye. All the world, but Greece, has sent him earth and water, because he is master of all lands and lord of all the seas. And now I have come to get earth and water from you. It is the Great King's command."

An angry roar went up from the crowd. Many men shook their fists at the strangers. The whole crowd pushed forward close to the platform, shouting angrily:

"Commands! Commands!"

"Take your commands back to your slaves, not to Athens," cried one man.

"Athens has no earth to spare," shouted another.

"The messenger has too much Athenian earth on his shoes now. Let him shake it off and begone," another called.

"Yes!" the whole crowd shouted. "Be off to your Great King! Athens does not want you. Go!" And they shook their fists.

The strangers on the platform gathered together and talked. The Athenian president looked on from his chair and smiled.

Another stranger came forward.

"Men of Athens," he began; but the crowd shouted him down.

The president stood up and raised his hand. "Let us hear this Persian and then answer him," he said.

So the people listened.

"Be careful what answer you send," said the Persian. "The Great King has many hands and many weapons. If his trumpet blows, warriors will run to him from the four ends of the earth. Those warriors will trample your little land into the sea. But the Great King is kind to his friends. For them sunshine falls from his eyes, and gold flows from his hand. You choose between death and the king's love."

"Death, then!" shouted the people.

A man came out of the crowd and ran up the steps upon the platform.

"Themistocles!" the people shouted. "Let us hear him!"

Themistocles caught up a crown of myrtle from the altar and put it upon his head. Then he turned quickly to the crowd. His eyes blazed.

"Men of Athens," he said; and his voice rang like a war-cry. "Remember the fair shores across the sea. There our kinsmen lived in beautiful cities. Their ships rode out to the corners of the world. Smoke rose from their altars to the gods. Freemen filled their market-places. Artists worked in their shops. Fearless soldiers walked the high walls and guarded the gates. Now those walls are flat. Those shops are empty. Those market-places are bare. Those altars are overturned. Those ships are sunk. Who has done these things? This Great King,

A PERSIAN AMBASSADOR

who commands us to give him earth and water. Will you make friends with him?"

"No!" shouted the crowd.

Themistocles pointed at the strange Greek.

"And this man," he said, "is from one of those ruined cities. Yet now he does the king's errands. He has put this Persian's words into Greek. Those words praised that Great King who has killed our kinsmen or made slaves of them. Those words were commands to us as though we were slaves. Shall any man dare to use our Greek language so? I move that this man be arrested and punished like a criminal."

The Athenian president leaped to his feet.

"All who think that this should be done will raise their hands."

There was a great uprush of hands, with a shout.

"It shall be done," said the president. "Guards, arrest this man. Persian, you have your answer. The meeting is over."

After that, Athens was a busy place. There were meetings often on the Pnyx hill. At one of them Themistocles said:

"Men of Athens, what we have done means war. We have expected this thing for a long time. We have watched the Great King's soldiers march up and down the lands across the sea. We have seen them beat down the walls of our neighbors. We ourselves went across and lent a hand. Nine years ago we burned the Persian's rich city. We have never expected the Great King to forget that. Have we not heard how a slave stands behind him at every meal and says, 'Master, remember the Athenians'? And have I not said to you, 'Athenians, remember the Persian war'? Has a man ever gone to the market-place to buy or to gossip without finding Themistocles there talking of the Persian war? Have you ever come to the assembly without hearing Themistocles say, 'We must have a port before the Persian war begins, and Piræus is the place'? At last the work started. Now we have a port at Piræus, and we have seventy ships on the sea. It is good, but it is not enough. We must have walls about our port. We must have more ships. We must be able to fight on the sea. For the Persians will come in boats. Our Athens lies on a plain here. Fields and gardens are all about her. The Persians will camp around her. They will eat our harvests. They will burn our houses. We shall die in our city. We must have ships to go to. We must have a safe place in which to leave our wives and children. Now Piræus is on a steep bluff. The sea goes around it almost all the way. We men can lie in our ships under the walls of Piræus and fight for our women. But more ships must be built. Piræus must be walled. There is not a moment to spare. We must all turn carpenters and shipbuilders and masons. Let us set to work."

THEMISTOCLES

So Athens was busy for a year. Then people began coming from Greek cities in the north.

"We are flying from the Persians," they said. "They are on their way here. They are breaking down the walls of our cities as they come."

Then one day men came from the island of Eubœa, just north of Athens. They were Athenians who had been in Eubœa for a little while.

"We have seen the Persians," they said. "They came in ships. They got out upon our land. We never saw such an army before. They covered the land. No city can stand before them. The towns of Eubœa are making a brave fight, but they will fall. We ran to tell you and to help. Make ready. The Persians will come here next."

The men of Athens held a great meeting. They chose their generals. They said to them:

"Call together all the men of Athens who are able to fight. Leave a few to guard the city. Take the others to meet the Persians. We must stop them here. They must not come upon Greek soil. Sparta will help us. Let us send a runner to tell her."

The next two days were busy ones. Pheidippides was off to Sparta to get help. The generals were drilling their army.

"But what can we do?" said a man in the market-place. "We are only a handful against a million. Sparta must send us all she can. And then we shall lose."

"What can we do?" cried another man. "Our best, and the gods will fight with us. This is their land as well as ours."

On the second day the guard at a gate blew his trumpet and called:

"Pheidippides is coming back. I see him running along the road near the river."

When men heard that, they began to run.

"Pheidippides!" they cried. "To the market-place! Hear his message. Pheidippides is back from Sparta."

So the word went. From all corners of the city men ran to the market-place. They crowded close around the doors of the officers' house. Pheidippides would come there to give his message. The crowd was silent. Men's faces were pale. They were thinking:

"Will Sparta come? Must we stand alone?"

At last Pheidippides came through the gate of the market. He dragged his feet in a slow run. His wet body glistened in the light. Dust was caked on his legs. His nostrils were spread. Men could hear his breath whistle through them. His lips were white and tight shut. His eyes were red. A man put out his arms, and Pheidippides fell into them.

"Sparta will not come," he said.

His voice was thick. Then he rested. Men turned to one another with pale faces.

"She will not come," they whispered.

Then they waited to hear more from Pheidippides.

"I ran to their market-place," he said. "Their kings and best men were there. I said: 'Athens asks you for help. The Persians are coming. The men of Eubœa are already made slaves, and their cities are burned. Help us!' But they turned slowly to talk among themselves. And one said to me: 'It is a long run; you must bathe and eat.' 'No, no!' I cried. 'Your answer!' But still they talked. At last they turned and said to me: 'There is no need for hurry. Our great festival of Apollo comes in a few days. We must wait for that. After that we will come.'

"I did not wait to hear more. Back I ran to Athens, over the mountains, down the valleys, through the rivers. And every hour my legs grew heavy, and my breath short, for anger at Sparta filled my throat, and my heart was cold with fear for Athens. At last I stumbled in a little stream, and I cried out: 'O gods of Olympus, help me!' And as I fell I saw a goat-beard moving in a little dim cave and I heard a shrill note of Pan's pipe. I lay trembling, afraid to look up. Then there was a quick stir through the bushes. I felt a rough hand on my head. At that touch fire rushed through my veins. I leaped up. Pan was gone, but his own strength was in me. My lungs were fresh. My legs were steady. My heart laughed. The rest of the way I ran like a wind to tell you: 'Fear not. We have a friend. Pan helps us. We win!' "

Then the men in that crowd threw up their hands and shouted:

"Pan and Athens!"

MARKET-PLACE IN ATHENS

The army of Athens was on the march. Behind them soldiers walked the wall of the Acropolis. The city streets were empty. The women and children sat trembling behind their shut doors. The old men talked in the market-place, waiting for news. Ahead of the army were the mountains and the pass. Beyond that were the Persians.

The Greeks marched for six hours. Then they came out from the pass. Before them lay a little plain. On one side of it rose a high mountain. On the other side was the sea. Here lay the Persian ships, drawn up on the sand. On the shore back of them were tents, stretching up and down the sea for miles. Some were black and mean looking. Some sparkled with cloth of gold. Some shone with bright colors. Some were made of skin. Among them bustled men in curious clothes.

Many of the Athenians had never seen the

Persians before. Now a noise of wonder went through their ranks. But they marched straight on. They kept close to the mountain. There was a wide hilltop at the foot. Here was a spring and an altar to Heracles. To this hilltop the Athenians marched, and here they set up their tents. After the work of making camp was over, men stood and looked down at the Persians and talked.

"Surely the whole world has poured soldiers into that camp," said one.

"And we alone stand against them," said another.

"We are not alone," said Pheidippides. "Pan fights with us,—Pan the gay, the strong, the bringer of fear."

"There is good omen in this place, too," said another man. "We fight at the altar of Heracles and on his ground. And here, hundreds of years ago, our king, Theseus, wrestled with a wild bull and won. We wrestle with the bull of Persia, and we shall win."

"Athene, too, will not desert us," another soldier said. "Has she not always fought with us? Is not her holy house in Athens? Did she not give us her own name? The gods are on our side."

"And yet," said the first man, "it is a sad thing that not one hand in all Greece is raised to help us. In her hundred cities men stand idle and watch us."

Late that afternoon the Athenians saw dust rise from the road they had just come over. Next they saw a glint of armor. By that time every man was looking.

A little column of soldiers was marching toward the camp. Who were they? They could not be foes from that direction. But what friends could they be?

"Sparta has changed her mind," some cried. "She has sent us soldiers."

"But what a handful!" others answered.

"They are not Spartans," a man said. "They have not the high helmets or the red chitons or the letter on their shields."

So men stood making guesses and changing them. The generals sent out a scout to see who the strangers were. The Athenians watched him running down the hill among the bushes. He kept hidden from the men marching. But as he went near, the Athenians saw him break from the bushes and run straight up the hill again. They heard him shouting before they could understand his words. But at last they made out:

"The men of Platæa! The men of Platæa! They are coming with a thousand soldiers to lend us a hand."

Then a great shout of joy rang from those Athenian throats. Men ran down the hill calling out. When the Platæans saw, they broke ranks and ran to meet their friends. All the way back men walked with their arms over each other's shoulders, and there were shouts of:

"Athens! Platæa! Little Platæa, the true-hearted!"

In the camp the Athenian generals met the

Platæan commander. They grasped his hands. Tears were in men's eyes.

"Athens sent her friend no message," said the Platæan. "Did you think we were not worth telling? It is true that our city is little and weak. But we shall never forget that day when we sat on the altar-steps at Athens and asked her for help. She raised us up and called us friends that day and fought our battle for us. And since then she has struck many a blow for us. Now we can help her. Our swords are few, but our hearts are full of love."

When the Athenians went to sleep that night, their faces shone with gladness. They had almost forgotten the Persians and were remembering their friend, little Platæa, the true-hearted.

For nine days the Athenians and Persians sat in their camps and looked at each other.

"The more often I see these Persians," said an Athenian, "the less I fear them. I think they are more slaves than soldiers."

"After this war," said another, "I will never wear a long chiton again. It is too like the Persian dress."

"After this war we shall all be Persian slaves," another soldier said.

"Faint-heart!" cried a dozen men.

"Faint-heart indeed!" he said. "I am not afraid of twice or three times our numbers. But look! The plain is flooded with men. There are spearmen and swordsmen. There are bowmen and slingers to shoot from afar. There are horsemen to run upon us and then be off before we can breathe. We have no bowmen and no horsemen. The enemy are ten times our number. I say, let us wait until Sparta comes to help."

"Wait for Sparta!" cried the others. "Wait for the Persians to burn Athens!"

"Half our generals think as I do," said the man.

"But Miltiades knows better," the others replied. "When the right time comes, he will lead us out. He will not wait for Sparta. And Themistocles is of the same mind. They are the men for Athens."

MILTIADES

On the ninth morning the Persians began to move. The ships were pushed off into the water. The horsemen saddled their horses and rode on board and sailed off. Then the footmen made ready to go into their ships.

Miltiades had called his Greeks into line. They stood on the hilltop waiting and looking at the Persians.

"We have frightened them away," men said. "They dare not try to march past us to Athens. They will sail around to the city. We must stop them. What will our command be?"

Some Persians stood in arms on guard. Others were getting into their boats. Off on the sea shone the sails of the ships that were carrying the horsemen away.

Then at last Miltiades gave the word to march. The Greek army moved down the hill in a long, thin line, five hundred men abreast. In the middle the line was only two or three men deep. It moved steadily ahead. Every man held his spear before him. His shield was tight to his left side. His sword swung at his knee. The helmets glistened. Dust rose behind the line. The men sang a war-song as they marched. Soon Miltiades gave another command. The trumpets blew. The men shouted the war-cry for Athens. Then they all broke into a run, still shoulder to shoulder.

The Persians were surprised. The guards gave the alarm. The others turned to look. Some leaped out of their boats. Then there was a rushing about. Men caught up their arms and fell into line. But the Greeks were upon them quickly. The Persian arrows had just begun to fly when the Greeks were already pushing with their spears and slashing with their swords.

The Persians were on the very shore. The sea was behind, the Greeks in front. So they fought for their lives, and they did many brave deeds. Their swords rang loud on the Greek armor. And from the back of their line their arrows dropped like stinging hail upon the heads of the Greeks. Few of the Persians wore armor. The Greek swords tore through their soft clothes and sank into their flesh. Yet they stood firm, and many a Greek and Persian fell together after a brave fight. But when a Persian in the front line died, another stepped forward and took his place; for they were many. New foes stepped out so fast that there was no time for the Greeks to take breath. They were wounded, their armor was slashed, their spears were broken, yet they kept up the fight; for they were thinking:

"These Persians will make us slaves, if they win. They will burn our homes. They will carry away our wives and children. We must drive them back."

And some things happened that put heart into the Greeks.

"Courage, friends," a man cried to his neighbors. "Did you not see Athene's helmet flash along the line? Did you not hear the whizzing of her spear?"

"Athene for Athens!" they shouted back; and courage leaped into their hearts.

"Pan! Pan!" cried Pheidippides. "He fights beside me. He has kept his promise."

"See! There is Heracles with his good club."

"The gods are with us," all men thought, and were glad.

So they pushed the Persians before them. Many they struck dead on the shore. Some fell into the sea. Most leaped into their boats and pushed off. Then the Athenians ran into the water after them. They caught hold of the ships and struck down the rowers and broke the oars and fought with the soldiers. The Persians struck bravely back, and many Greeks dropped into the sea and died. But some boats the Greeks burned there on the shore, while the others sailed away. At last only the dead warriors and the burning ships and the Greeks were left on the battle-field.

Then the Athenians rested and looked about. Thousands of men lay dead on the plain,—Greeks and Persians.

"This is the price we pay for our city," Miltiades said. "But we must be ready for them."

He left one company to bury the dead. The others he led back to Athens. Their armor was cut and dented. Some men carried Persian swords or shields, because their own had been lost in the fight. On many bare arms and legs were wounds, sometimes wrapped with rags of Persian dress. It was a broken army. But there was a joy in their hearts such as they had never felt before. They had done a thing such as no other army had ever done. They had beaten the army of the Great King.

When they came near Athens, they saw the Persian boats coming towards Piræus. But at the sight of the Athenian armor the Persians turned away. They had had enough of fighting. They sailed back across the sea to Persia, and Athens was at rest.

Then the first thing was to raise a mound of earth over the dead warriors. Some people had said:

"Let us bring them back to the city and bury them there. All the other soldiers who have died for Athens lie over there in our cemetery."

But other men said:

"No. Let them lie on the battle-field. No other men ever fought such a battle. They are the first Greeks to meet the Persians. They are heroes."

So there on the plain of Marathon they raised a

great mound over their brave soldiers. On the top they put ten stone columns and cut on them the names of the men buried there. They raised another mound over the Platæans. And they cut their names on a column.

A SOLDIER OF MARATHON

"Let no man ever forget," said the Athenians, "that the Platæans came to Athens in her need and did brave deeds at Marathon."

At the next meeting in the Pnyx they voted for a festival of Marathon.

"Our children and their children for hundreds of years must not forget Marathon," the people said. "It is the best battle that ever was fought. It saved Greece. Every year we will hold a Marathon festival. On that day we will sacrifice to the gods in thanksgiving. And our herald shall pray, and these shall be his words, 'May the gods bless the Athenians and the Platæans!' And on that day we will burn sacrifices on those mounds as on holy altars. Our soldiers shall drill there on that day, looking at the mounds of those heroes. So they shall remember to be brave like the men who died there for Athens."

It was in the middle of the forenoon several months after the battle of Marathon. The market-place was full of people. Flower-girls were running about with their baskets.

"Roses, roses! Violets from the plains! Crocuses from the road to Piræus! Flowers! Buy, buy!"

Rough fellows, in short brown or gray chitons, stood by their little tables and beat upon gongs and cried:

"Fish, fish! Fresh fish! Caught but an hour ago! Come buy!"

Bankers sat on their benches behind their little tables covered with boxes and coins. They were changing money for visitors from foreign cities, and they were lending to gay young men, who dropped the coins into their bags and were off, laughing.

A pottery-seller had his little table full of red and black vases.

"Come buy a Marathon vase," he called, "painted with pictures of our glorious battle."

And among those dozens of tables and crying merchants walked the men of Athens. Their slaves followed with baskets and money-bags. Some were buying vegetables and fruits and wines and meat and bread and cakes for dinner. Others were buying clothes and sandals; others, vases, jewels, lamps, olive oil. So the baskets of the slaves were filled.

"This sight delights my eyes," said a man who stood talking to friends. "Peace is the real glory of a land. We have driven out the Persians; now we can rest."

JUGS, DECORATED BY VASE PAINTERS

"Rest?" cried a man who had just come up. "Rest with no wall about Athens? Rest with our port unfinished? Rest with no ships to meet our foes on the sea? Are the Persians driven out? Only driven back to make better plans. How long do you think it will be before we see the water white with Persian sails and feel our land tremble under Persian feet? Rest? There is not an hour to spare. Are the men of Athens mad to think of resting now? We can rest when Persia is dead."

"Oh, Themistocles raving again!" laughed one of the men. "You are a skeleton at the feast, Themistocles. Three men cannot stand together anywhere in Athens without having you come up and rave about the Persians and the work to be done."

"A skeleton at the feast?" cried Themistocles. "You need one. You have drunk the wine of victory. It has made you drowsy. Must I frighten you to work?

The king of Persia can get together enough soldiers to cover our land. And do you think he will not do it? Is he not ashamed of Marathon? Will he not try to wipe out that disgrace? How can we win against him? His weakest point is his navy. Persians are not sailors. He must borrow his ships and crews from lands that he conquers. Those men will fight from fear of him. Can such men win against men who fight for their own dear country? So I say: Let us build ships. Let us all go aboard and leave an empty land for the Persian army. But let us meet the ships on the sea, and we shall win. We have seventy boats now. We must have two hundred."

"Ho-o!" laughed the men about Themistocles; for a crowd had gathered to listen. "Two hundred ships of war! Where can you get the money? Where can you get the men to do the work?"

"I know of ten rich men," Themistocles replied, "who have already said: 'We will each pay for the building of a ship.' "

A fish-seller put his hands on his hips and raised his eyebrows and gave a long whistle.

"Nothing stingy about that!" he said.

"No," cried a potter. "But they are rich. We poor men have nothing to give."

"Have you not?" cried Themistocles.

He pointed to the east.

"Off there are the silver mines of Athens," he said. "Rich men work them and pay rent—to whom? To you and me, the freemen of Athens. The rent will soon be due. Will you spend it for Athens?"

"No!" cried a blacksmith. "I need it to buy a new bellows."

"You will need no bellows, Ariston," said Themistocles, "when the Persians have set fire to Athens."

"The Persians!" laughed a dozen men. "When our children are men, they can take care of the Persians. Now they are far off."

Then the company broke up. Themistocles walked slowly away. His mouth was set hard. There was a frown on his forehead.

"They must do it," he was thinking. "How can I plan it? They must listen."

He had done more than he thought that day. Those men went away scoffing. But they could not forget Themistocles' words. Some talked together of the matter afterwards.

And Themistocles was in the market-place every day. And always he talked about the war, the walls, the navy.

"Here comes the Athenian navy," men used to say of him when they saw him coming.

"If you meet this man at a banquet," a young fop once said, "he will not touch the lyre and sing of love or of beauty or of the gods, as other men do. He talks of the Athenian navy. If you go to the market-place to have a pleasant chat in a perfumer's shop, in will come Themistocles and make your head ache with the Athenian navy. I am coming to dream at night of him and his navy."

"And there are worse things to dream of," replied a friend of Themistocles.

"Yes," answered another man. "Now that this trouble with Ægina has come, a navy would not be a bad thing for Athens."

So the talk grew.

Again there was a meeting on the Pnyx hill. The sacrifices and prayers were over. Then Themistocles stepped upon the platform and put the myrtle crown upon his head. Above him to right and left stretched the crowd of Athenian men. Before Marathon it had been a crowd with long robes and long hair and flashing jewels. Now it was a crowd with close-cropped hair and short chitons and bare legs,—a crowd of active men, of haters of Persia.

Themistocles' voice rang out:

"Men of Athens, what will you do? Our sacred ship and our holy priests are not safe on the seas. We send them to the temple of Poseidon for the great festival. The men of Ægina hide on our shores and steal our priests. Our merchants sail out from Piræus in ships loaded with rich stuffs. The men of Ægina lie in wait, sink the ships, carry home the rich goods. And have you heard the talk of the traders from across the sea? The Great King is mad with anger. They say: 'He will conquer Greece yet. He has called a new army together. The whole land of Persia clangs with arms and marching men. This time the king himself will lead his army.'

"These things are not news to you now. You have talked them over in the market-place during the last few days. What shall we do? Ægina is an island. Her men are at home on the sea as well as on the land. There is but one way to meet them,—in ships. The Persians will burn our land. Where shall we stand then? In ships.

"There lie in our treasure-house now chests of money, the rent from our silver mines. Athens is ready to divide it among you. Will you have it to buy clothes that shall burn in Persian fire? Will you have it to buy wheat to eat while the men of Ægina drink the wine that our ships take to sea? Will you have it to lay away in money-chests for Persians to break open? Or will you build ships with it, to be a strong right arm for Athens?—ships that will drive the men of Ægina home; ships that will keep our waters safe and bring rich traders to our port; ships that will save our wives and children and land from Persia. I move that the money from the silver mines be spent for building a navy to save Athens."

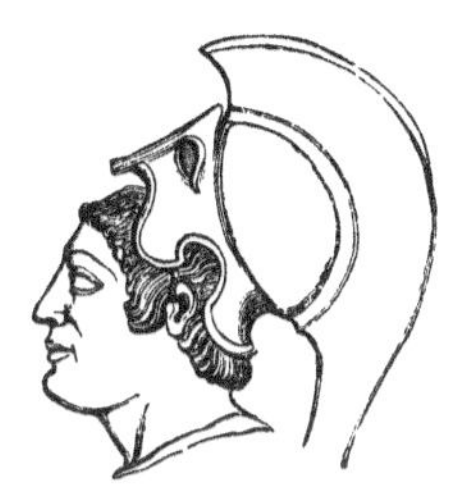

A SOLDIER OF ÆGINA

The president asked for the vote. Then the men of Athens forgot their little wishes and their stinginess and their poverty. They remembered only their dear

Athens,—her honor, her glory, her need, her danger. They voted to give their money to her.

Attica was a busy land. The pine forests on the mountains were full of men. There were the ringing of axes and the crashing of falling trees. Long lines of mules dragged logs down the hills and across the plains to the seashore. Here was the noise of saw and hammer, where carpenters were building ships. Here, too, was the smoke of fire, where blacksmiths were making the sharp beaks of ships. Clumsy mule-carts creaked across the plains, from the stone quarries to Piræus. There stonecutters and masons were building docks. Housebuilders, too, were busy. For news of what Athens was doing spread through Greece. Many men came seeking work. These foreigners built their houses at Piræus. So a busy little city began to grow up here.

Off the shore were little boats going about all day. They seemed to carry nothing and to go nowhere. Aboard them were the young men of Athens, learning to be sailors. The boats were always being turned about; the sails were always being raised or lowered.

On a certain day, after three or four months of this work, one of these little boats came alongside a pier. Two young men leaped out. Their faces were tanned. Their short chitons were water-splashed. Their eyes were glad.

"O ho!" cried one in a gay voice, breaking into a run. "The sea! The sea! It is a fine thing."

The two young men ran along the pier, side by side.

"I used to think it shameful for a man's hands to smell of ropes and oars," said the first; "but now, Milon, I am as proud of that smell as of the oil of Olympia."

ONE OF THE TEMPLES OF POSEIDON

"Think of the days," answered Milon, "when we used to spend half our time in the gymnasium. The disc, the spear, the boxer's thongs, the race-course, the jumping weights,—they gave us strong muscles and quick eyes. But this, Demipho! This is striving with the gods themselves. Will Hermes blow our ship north? We make it go south. Will Poseidon beat her against the rocks? We guide her off. Athenians have been landsmen. These little islands have lorded it over the sea. Let them be careful! Athens is learning to pull the oar and work the sail. We have already made Ægina smart."

"But Persia!" said Demipho. "Shall we be able to hold out against her? King Xerxes builds a bridge a mile long. He sets his slaves to work, and in a few months he has dug a trench from sea to sea for his ships to sail through. His army has been three years coming together. He has said that he will not rest until he has burned Athens. What can we do against such a king?"

"Themistocles will find a way," replied Milon.

"True," Demipho answered. "What can he not do? He has built a fleet and has turned farmers and merchants into sailors."

The two young men were walking along a country road. Before them stood up the steep Acropolis hill, with its temples. Other hills clustered around it. The houses lay among them. The young men came to the foot of the Pnyx. Streams of men were pouring toward it. All were talking excitedly. The words "Persians," "Xerxes," were spoken often. They all walked up the hill and showed little tickets to the keeper of the gate. Those tickets of sheepskin told that the men who held them had a right to go to the meetings of Athens. So they all passed in.

After the sacrifice, Themistocles went upon the platform to speak.

"Men of Athens," he said, "the Great King is coming. He sits on his throne and sees his army drill. He waits only for the great bridge to be finished. Then he will cross the water into Greece. Again he has sent for earth and water. Some of our neighbors have given them to him. But most Greeks are still freemen. They have sent the messengers home empty-handed. What are those Greek freemen to do? There are a hundred cities and more in Greece. Every one stands alone, a jealous foe of every other. But can they stand so against Persia and her million soldiers? We have enemies in Ægina and in Sparta. Our hearts have been hot with anger against both. But would you have Persians make slaves of Spartans? Would you have Athens safe and see Delphi burned or see Persians run at Olympia? We are all Greeks and brothers. Shall we not stand shoulder to shoulder against Persia? I propose a meeting of all the lovers of Greece. Let it be at Corinth, in the middle of Greece. I move that we send messengers to every city, telling them of this plan."

The men of Athens voted for that motion.

On the day set, the wisest men from those Greek cities came together at Corinth. Themistocles spoke:

"The first thing to say is that we are all friends. There are men here from cities that were once foes of Athens. We are foes no longer. We have enough of them in the Persian camp. This is no time to remember little things. There is only one thing to remember,—Greece."

And those men vowed that all quarrels should stop. Men talked kindly together who had not long ago raised spear against each other. So they began to plan what to do.

"The Great King sits in his camp across the sea," one Greek said, "waiting for his bridge. If we knew his numbers and the kind of weapons and men, we could plan better. Let us send spies to steal into the camp and look about."

It was done. The Greeks waited many days for the return of those spies. When they did come, they told this story:

"We came to the rich city of the king and were looking about us. But the generals found us out and led us away to kill us. At the last moment the king sent, saying: 'Bring the spies to me.' So we went.

"There he sat like the statue of a god, high on a golden chair. He himself, in purple robe, was all a glitter of gold and jewels. About him stood a thousand servants. They carried the king's napkin, the king's parasol, the king's perfume bottle, the king's fan, the king's cup, the king's wine bottle, the king's hand-basin. They knelt to offer him drink. They bowed to the floor when they spoke to him. 'Why are you here?' the king asked us. 'We have come to see your army and to tell the Greeks about it,' we answered, expecting to die. Then the king called his guards and said: 'Show these men about. Let them see everything,—my horsemen, my bowmen, my spearmen, my slingers, my runners, my chariots, my mules, my stores of food, my chests of gold.' So we walked for a whole day through that camp, seeing new things always. Never before had we seen so many men. It was like twenty Greek cities put into one. Surely we cannot fight with that army."

But men who heard answered: "It is better to die with a sword in your hand and in the smile of the gods than to live to carry the king's fan. Why should we be discouraged? True, half of Greece lies trembling under the Great King. But we are still free. Zeus and Apollo and Athene still sit on Olympus. Have their arms lost their strength? Do not their arrows shoot as straight, and are their spears not as sharp, as when they helped the Greeks against Troy?"

So with brave hearts they set to planning. Not long after that, word came that the Persian army had crossed the great bridge.

"And so large was the army," men said, "that for seven days and nights the bridge was full of soldiers marching. There were men from all parts of the world: Greeks from across the sea in their bronze armor, Arabs on horses, men from India in white robes, savages in skins. Now they are marching down toward Greece. The ships are sailing along the coast near the army."

Then the men at Corinth said to Sparta:

"You are best in war. Send an army to the narrow pass at Thermopylæ to stop the Persians. We will send the ships to lie near that army to stop the fleet."

But Sparta sent only a few men under Leonidas. All the ships, however, sailed north, ready for work. And half of them all were Athenian, and Themistocles was with them. They lay waiting for several days. And while they waited, their courage faded away. Many captains said:

"Let us sail south again. We cannot meet the Persians here. We are too far from home."

So Themistocles was very busy. To one man he must say this thing, to another one that. Some he laughed at, others he threatened, trying to put courage into their hearts. And he succeeded. He kept the fleet together.

At last the Persian ships came into sight, and with them came the news:

"Poseidon has not forgotten the Greeks. He has sent storms that wrecked many Persian ships."

Now there lay the Persian fleet a few miles away. Here lay the Greeks looking at it.

"What is there terrible about those ships?" the Greek sailors said among themselves. "How will those men fight? Do they know how to handle a ship? Let us try them."

So finally they fought, two hundred ships against a thousand. Three different times they had little battles, and in every battle the Greeks did brave work. At night a storm helped the Greeks by wrecking more of the Persian ships. The Greek boats were safe in the harbor out of the waves.

But the last fight was a hard one. More than twenty Greek ships were sunk. And that same night the news came of the lost battle at Thermopylæ. Then even Themistocles said:

"Let us fight no more. Our ships need repairing. Thermopylæ is lost. We cannot keep this north country. We must let the Persians have it. We must save the southern part. But let no man think that we have been beaten in this sea-fight. Wrecked Persian ships and dead Persian sailors tell that we were not afraid, and that we know how to handle a fleet. Greece has no cause to be ashamed of us. We will meet the foe again."

AN OFFERING TO APOLLO AT THE TEMPLE OF DELPHI

A while before the sea-battle, the people of Athens had sent to Delphi to ask Apollo about the war. This was the message they received:

"When all inside Athens is lost, Zeus will give you wooden walls to save you. Do not wait for the army marching down, but turn and flee. You will still be able to face them. O divine Salamis, you will cause men to die whether the harvest is gathered in or not."

The Athenians could not understand this message. Some said,

"What are the wooden walls?"

Others answered:

"That must be the old wooden wall around the Acropolis. Are not our holiest temples there? Is not the holy wooden statue of Athene there? That is the place for us to flee to."

But others laughed at that.

"Impossible!" they said. "Not half the people of Athens could be crowded upon the Acropolis. Apollo would not give such advice."

"Salamis will cause men to die," men repeated, thinking. "That must mean that we are to flee to Salamis. Then the Persians will come and kill us."

"No, no!" others cried. "Zeus will save us and our children."

"Why are you sad?" Themistocles said. "This is a good message. Is not the island of Salamis bare and rocky? Yet Apollo calls it divine. What makes it divine? The good fortune that will happen there. 'Zeus will give us wooden walls,' Apollo says. But where? We are not to wait for the Persians, but to flee away. We must flee to Salamis. 'But there is no wooden wall at Salamis,' you say. Look at the sea. There lie our ships of wood, strong walls for brave men. What Apollo means is: 'Flee from Athens. Go aboard your ships. Meet the foe at Salamis. You will win a glorious battle.' "

But some people doubted.

"Themistocles can never see anything but his ships," they said.

Others frowned, saying,

"Apollo would not tell us to leave our homes, our father's graves, our temples, our holy statues."

All this happened before the war began.

After those first sea-battles were over, the Greek fleet came south. Themistocles returned to Athens. He found the people unhappy.

"What shall we do?" they said to him. "Thermopylæ is lost. The Persian army is marching down upon us. The Persian fleet is sailing down. Sparta will not send us help. She will take the Greek fleet and the Greek army farther south and leave us to the Persians."

"And she will do right," Themistocles replied. "No army can hold our land now against the Persians. We must give it up. But there is a new Athens built for you. Will you scorn it? Has it not made you proud of it in these last few days? You dread to leave your father's graves. Is that not better than to make Persian slaves of your fathers' sons? Some time we will come back and raise new stones at those graves and write on them, 'Fathers of the men who beat the Persians on the sea.' Do you dread to leave the temples? But the gods are not chained to their altars. Is it not Athene who sends victory to Athens in war? Then was she not with us in these battles on the sea?"

"But our women and children cannot go on shipboard," men said. "What will happen to them?"

That was a hard question. But in a few days word came from the city of Trœzen:

"Athens and Trœzen are friends from of old. Let us keep your women and children. They shall be the guests of our city. They shall stay with us until you have some place for them. We will send your boys to school. Your children shall play in our parks. They will not be unhappy."

For days men talked about all these things in the streets. It was a sad city. But at last they voted to go away.

THE ATHENIANS FLEEING TO THEIR SHIPS

When the last day came, the streets of Athens were a strange sight. Men, women, and children, rich men and slaves, were walking to the sea. Every man carried a load of his most precious things. Mules, packed with clothes and furniture, followed. Wooden carts creaked along. At the shore all was thrown out upon the ground and loaded into boats. Early in the morning the priests had taken the most holy statues and dishes from the temples. They were now on a ship sailing to Salamis. Some of the wise old men went with them.

"In Salamis is the new Acropolis," they said.

As the people walked the streets, some wept, and some cried out to the gods. Some looked back and waved farewell at the empty city. Some squared their shoulders as if for the battle ahead. One gay company of young men ran through the streets and up to the temple of Athene on the Acropolis. Here they hung up the bridles of their horses, saying,

"We change horses for ships."

Shields hung over the columns in the porch of the temple. They had been won in old battles by Athenian warriors. Each young man took one down and put it upon his arm. Then they ran down the hill and off toward the sea, shouting,

"Victory for the new Athens!"

The Greek fleet lay off the shores of Salamis, waiting. Then one day a man came rowing toward them, calling:

"News from Athens!"

Eagerly the sailors pulled him over the side of Themistocles' boat.

"What is your news?" they cried; and their faces grew white.

"The Persians have marched down from Thermopylæ," he said. "They have burned Thespiæ. They have burned Platæa. The great army marched

ATHENE

through our land of Attica. The grain fields burned behind them. Men and women fled before them. The temples of Athens are ashes. Xerxes and his army sleep in our houses. But a few of us gave trouble at the Acropolis. We stayed there when you went because we thought Apollo meant that. But the Persians shot burning arrows, and our wooden walls fell in fire. But even then the enemy could not get up to us, for we rolled great rocks down the steep sides. But at last a few crawled up where we had no guards. Then some of us died fighting. Some ran to the holy altar of Athene, but the Persians killed them there. When I saw that the fight was lost, I ran to tell you. I went down the underground stair and through the cave. Surely Athene guarded me as I stole around the great army. As I left the shore, I turned back and saw the roof of the temple fall and the flames shoot up. A smoke hangs over all Athens. She is dead and buried on her holy hill."

Then all that shipload of men groaned and could not speak a word. But men from other ships were shouting questions, and at last the answer came,

"Athens is burned, Xerxes has come."

Then suddenly here and there sails were raised, and ships moved off.

"What are you doing?" men from other boats called.

"We are going home," came the answer. "Only fools will stay."

"Only cowards will go," shouted an Athenian.

"Have you no gods to make you ashamed?"

"Do you call yourselves Greeks? Bah! They are Persians."

Such were the cries that came from the Athenian boats and from some others. Yet many were silent, wishing to run away.

The captains came together to plan what to do. A Spartan was general. They met on his boat. There was a long talk. At last the meeting ended, and Themistocles came rowing back to his own boat. His brow was heavy. His face was gloomy. He went aboard and walked to the bow. Here he stood looking off into the dark, towards Athens. His men watched him, and their hearts grew sick. After a while an old man, his friend, went close to him.

"What do they plan to do?" he asked in a low voice.

"To go south and wait before Corinth," Themistocles answered, without turning.

"Do you know what will happen then?" said the friend. "If we leave Salamis, we shall never fight for any country. Every ship will go to its own city. Then not only will Athens be ashes, but Greeks will be slaves. Go to the Spartan again."

Without a word, Themistocles walked to the side of the ship and got into his boat.

"To the general's ship," he said to the rowers.

As he came near, he called out,

"I must see the general on business."

"Come aboard," was shouted back.

So Themistocles went aboard. He sat with the general alone in the bow of the boat.

"If we leave Salamis, we shall scatter to the four winds," he said. "The men are afraid. You know that. They will fly home if the flock moves. Call the captains together again. Let us talk further."

For an hour Themistocles urged. At last the Spartan sent messengers to call the captains. They came, and at once Themistocles began to talk.

"Apollo has lent him his own tongue," said a man.

"But why should this man talk?" cried another, mockingly. "He should have no vote. He has no country."

Then Themistocles turned, and his eyes blazed.

"Have we Athenians no country?" he said. "Our city is in ashes, but look!" He pointed to the Athenian ships. "There is our country. Of those four hundred ships, two hundred are Athenian."

Then he turned again to the Spartan general.

"If you stay here, we can save Greece. Apollo has promised Athens victory at Salamis. If you do not stay, then bid farewell to us and our two hundred ships. We will go to find a new home far west."

That threat won. At last the captains voted to stay.

On the next morning the Greeks saw the Persian fleet come sailing in from the north. All the host of the army, too, marched down the shore from Athens.

"They have come to see us die," cried out a Corinthian.

The Greeks lay facing the hosts of the Persians, while the king took time to hold a meeting and look over his ships. And all the time fear grew in the hearts of the Greeks.

"We were fools to listen to Themistocles," men said. "He stays for the sake of Athens. We shall all die here for the sake of that dead city."

So men stood on their ships, scowling and talking together. By night their fears had grown so great that they called a meeting. The captains were crowded on the deck of the general's ship. They looked out on the Greek fleet as they talked. Far off, the Persian ships lay in the moonlight. They stretched for miles along the shore.

"We will not stay here," the captains cried, "to be carved up by Persian swords."

Then followed a long, angry talk. Once a sailor called Themistocles out. He soon came back with another man. The stranger said to the company:

"Some of you know me. I am Aristides, the Athenian. I have been an exile from Athens. But I have come back now to fight for her. Are you talking of going away? It is too late. I have just come from Ægina. I could barely steal through the line of Persian ships. They are drawn up before you in a close half-circle. Behind you a half-circle of land shuts you in. You are in a trap. You must fight."

There was some grumbling then, but most men lost their fear when it came to the touch. Every captain went back to his ship and made ready for a fight in the morning.

"Themistocles looked as though what Aristides told was no news to him," one man said.

"Very likely his finger was in it somewhere," another answered.

And indeed it was. When he saw from the talk of the captains that they meant to go away, he sent a messenger to Xerxes, saying:

"I come from the general of the Greeks. He is a friend to the Great King. The Greeks are going away, for they are afraid. If you would catch them, shut them in with your ships. So you can best conquer them and win great glory."

And so the king had done.

In the morning the Greeks saw the Persian ships around them. Back on the shore sat the king, high on his golden throne. And all about him glittered his soldiers. On the rocks of Salamis stood the old men of Athens, and some of the women and children. All these foes and friends were looking down on the little Greek fleet.

XERXES, THE GREAT KING ON HIS THRONE

"It is like a great theater," said an Athenian. "We are the actors. There is the audience. Who will clap their hands, and who will weep?"

"And there is another audience," said a man. He pointed to the sky. "There sit all the gods watching."

Soon the fighting men of the Greeks were called together on a few ships about the general. Then some of the captains spoke to them. Themistocles said:

"For what do we fight? Not only for Athens, not only for Sparta, nor Corinth, nor Ægina, but for all of Greece. Do you fear those Persians? Do you think that the gods of Greece will let them make slaves of the people that are dear to Olympus?"

Then the fighting men went back to their boats. Most of the Greek ships had three rows of oars, one above the other. A man sat at every oar. Above the rowers was a deck. Along the sides went a bulwark. Behind this stood the fighting men, fifteen or twenty for every boat.

At last the trumpet blew, and the ships were rowed forward. Then there was such a fight as Greece had never had before. "The trumpet, with its clang, fired the hearts of the Greeks. Swiftly they came on with dashing oars. The Persians could hear a mighty shout and a song:

" 'O sons of the Greeks,
For the freedom of your land and the freedom of your sons,
For the shrines of the gods, for the graves of your sires!
All now hangs on the fight.'

"Then ship dashed her brazen prow at ship. At first the Persians stood against the foe, but their thousand ships were crowded in the narrow sea. They struck each other with their own brazen beaks and broke their own oars. And the Greek vessels hit them and broke their oars and overturned their ships. The water could not be seen, it was so filled with wrecks and men. The sea and the air were filled with wailing. The Persian boats that could, rowed away in flight. King Xerxes went mourning home."

So the story was told in a play years after the battle.

Salamis did not end the war. Part of the king's army stayed to fight it out. There was war on land for a year after that. Again the Persians camped in Athens.

But at last the Greeks won a great battle. Then the Persians who were left marched home, never to trouble Greece again.

So the men and women of Athens went back to their city. But it was no longer a city. The temples were piles of blackened stones. Old homes were changed to a cartload of ashes. For miles about, the fields and hillsides were black.

"Men of Athens, do you see your work?" Themistocles had said. "There is no time for mourning. How long before those black fields shall be yellow with grain? How long before those black hillsides shall laugh with purple grapes? How long before the black banks of Cephissus, there, shall be green with olive trees? Were the vines and the trees that men burned those that your great-grandfathers planted? What of that? They had lived long enough. These new vines and trees will be the vines and the trees that the men of Salamis planted. Will not your children's children be more proud of that? Ages ago Athene brought an olive tree out of the ground for us. We guarded it lovingly in the yard of her temple. That holy tree burned in the Persian fire. But Athene did not mourn. Athenians offered sacrifice to her there on the ashes of her temple and her tree, and lo! from the old roots a new sprout shot up tall as a man. From that new sprout you shall get slips for new orchards, from Athene you shall get the courage to build a new city. See, yonder the unfinished walls of Piræus still stand. Our ships are out on the sea keeping Persians behind their walls. Let us have a place to receive those brave ships, when they return. There is much to do: our own homes to rebuild; our orchards and vineyards to plant; the walls of Athens to set up; our harbor to finish; the temples of the gods to make anew. Which work shall come first, yours or that of Athens?"

PIRÆUS; ATHENS IN THE DISTANCE; THE LONG WALLS

Their work shows what their answer was. Two years after the war there was a strong wall around Athens. It was thirty feet high, with gates and towers. Another like it went around Piræus. A pair of long walls stretched between the two cities. Perhaps altogether there were fifteen miles of wall. For some of the time men had worked on it night and day. They had put into it things that they loved: the columns of the fallen temples; broken altars of the gods; the gravestones of their fathers.

"We cannot wait for the quarries," men said. "Let us take whatever we can lay our hands on. Sparta will stop our work, if we do not hurry. She is jealous. She would keep us a weak village. She wishes to be the only strong city. She may even send an army to stop us. But while Themistocles is in Sparta, we must work. He will hold her off with some wily words until we have finished."

So they worked with their hands, while Themistocles worked for them with his head, and they built those great walls.

Themistocles had been dead for many years. Athens was the richest and most beautiful city in Greece. At Piræus marble docks and storehouses lined the shore, and they were full of grain and precious goods from afar. The city was built close, with fine houses along broad, straight streets. Here and there temples shone with soft colors.

A straight road stretched through the low country to Athens. On either side of it stood up high stone-walls. Even in war men could walk safely from town to port.

At the gate of Athens the wall spread out and went in a ragged circle about the city. Crooked streets wound among the little bare hills. Plain houses sat close together along both sides. The men of Athens had spent their time and their money on the buildings of Athens, not on their own houses.

The market-place was fenced about with offices of marble, with wide porches before them. On the walls were painted pictures that told of the glories of Athens. One was of the battle of Marathon. Before the porches stood statues of heroes.

The city was dotted over with temples (a hundred or more),—temples of Heracles, of Theseus, of Athene, of Apollo, of Zeus, of Hermes, of Artemis, of Poseidon.

Some of these buildings were large, with columns all about them. Some were small, with only one door. But all of them were marble, and most of them had painted bas-reliefs and statues. And inside of all were wonderful gifts of gold and of ivory and of bronze, marble statues, vases, tablets, tripods. At almost every street corner stood a statue of some god or hero.

Just outside the wall was the burying-ground, where lay the heroes of Athens. And over every grave was a beautiful stone. There was carved a bas-relief of the dead person, showing him doing something that he had loved to do. The reliefs were painted in the colors of life. Often, too, gold necklaces or bracelets or head-bands or bronze swords or spear-points glistened on them.

In the middle of this beautiful city arose the Acropolis. Down one corner of the hill stretched the wide theater, with its marble seats. On the north side was the cave of Pan.

In most places the sides of the Acropolis were steep, bare rock. But all the western end was a rich shrine of marble road and columns and roofs and bronze doors. The flat top was a grove of statues and lovely things that people had given to the gods, and out of this forest rose two temples and a great bronze Athene.

The people of this wonderful city were holding a meeting on the Pnyx hill, as they had done in the days of Themistocles. A man, crowned with myrtle, was speaking from the platform.

EXILE OF THEMISTOCLES

"In return for our help against Persia, the islands of the sea pour gold into our treasure-house. Our navy is the defender of Greece. Who built that navy? Our ships sail all seas and bring back to us the wealth of the world. Who made us sailors? Look from this hill. Here circles our wall, and yonder stretches our walled road to Piræus. Who built those walls and planned that port? Far off you can see Salamis. There stands the monument which tells that Greece drove Persia from the sea. Who won that battle? A man spent his life to do these things. He dreamed of Athens by night and worked for her by day. And because he was a little vain and not smooth-spoken, our fathers exiled him from this Athens that he built up from ashes. Perhaps he had worse faults. Men say so. He went to Persia after Athens pushed him out. But has a Persian king no work that an honest man can do? Those who knew Themistocles best say that never once did he lose his love for Athens or plan harm to her. Indeed, some men say that he killed himself when the Great King asked him to do that. Themistocles had his faults, but can we not forget them? We have forgotten brave deeds long enough. Our city is full of statues, pictures, temples, tombs, that tell of the glories of that Persian war. Miltiades lies in our burying-ground. A tomb tells his name and his deed. His statue stands by our city hearth. Every soldier of that war has our honor. How long shall Themistocles be forgotten? How long shall he lie in Persian soil? Let him come back to this Athens that he loved and built. Let his tomb stand where he loved most to be—at Piræus, where boats go in and out, where our ships of war lie, where Salamis looks across. That tomb will add glory to our land."

So it was done, and Themistocles came home.

PHIDIAS AND THE PARTHENON

The night before, Athene's birthday had come. Nobody in Athens slept on that night. Around every temple door the street was loud with singing voices and dancing feet. It was bright with fluttering robes and flaring torches, and sweet with waving smoke of incense.

In front of one door danced a chorus of men. They were in armor, as if they had come from a fight. The bronze glinted in the torchlight. People pressed about in a close circle. Their eager eyes watched the dancers. Slaves held the smoking torches above their masters' heads. The voices that had shouted the battle-cry were now singing:

"Of Pallas Athene, the savior of cities, I sing,
Dread goddess, who has in her charge the works of war,
Of falling towns and of battles and battle-din,
Who saves the hosts as they go to the fight or return;
O hail, Athene! and give to us joy and good luck."

"Athene!" shouted the crowd.

"And we are her chosen warriors," said one man to another.

"Come to the altar of Here," said a man to his

friend. "My daughter dances there with the other priestesses."

GREEK GIRLS DANCING

They struggled through the moving crowds in the crooked streets. They groped their way through the dark, empty places. At last they came to another crowd, with the glare of torches around it. Flames leaped up, smoke waved above a thousand heads with their white fillets. Behind were the white temple columns, and at each side stretched the dark street. Here young girls were singing and helping the song with whirling bodies and clashing cymbals.

"Of fairest Athene I sing,
The gray-eyed, the wise.
She was not born as others are born.
She did not grow as others have grown;
But she sprang full grown, full armed,
From the head of Zeus,
And the gods stood about and watched with awe.

"Quickly she leaped from the head
Of the counselor Zeus,
Shaking her spear and flashing her mail
Till high Olympus trembled in dread.
And the wide earth shook below

At the maiden's strength,
And the dark sea boiled and broke in foam.

"Apollo, the glorious god,
Reined in his steeds
Till the maiden laid off her armor of gold,
While her father watched proudly the
    counselor Zeus.
So hail to thee, goddess Athene,
Daughter of Zeus!
So hail to thee, savior, the gray-eyed, the wise!"

In the market-place, too, thousands of torches flared and smoked. A great space in the center was roped off and empty. But watchers pressed against the rope and crowded together all the way back to steps and porches. Some had even climbed to the low roofs and were looking down on the unsteady lights and moving heads. At last a chorus of boys began singing and dancing in the space roped off. They told the story of the naming of Athens: how in the olden days Athene and Poseidon together came to the city. They went to the Acropolis, where all men were met to buy and sell and talk. Those gods found a nameless town. Each said: "Call your city after me, and I will give you a precious gift." Then Poseidon struck the rock with his trident. Out

POSEIDON

leaped the first horse, and the people were afraid. But Athene made an olive tree shoot softly up, and the people said: "We will have Athene for our goddess." So Athens was named.

The shrill music of a flute pierced far past the market. As the boys of the chorus sang to its sound, they acted the story: Zeus' headache; the swing of Hephæstus' hammer; Athene's leaping out; the raised hands and backward steps of the surprised gods; the glad running of Iris to tell the news.

ATHENE

At the end of the dance the noise of clapping hands and the cries of "Good, good!" carried far through the open air.

"The lads did well, Lacon," said a man. "I saw your son among them. He is a handsome boy."

"Every day for a month," replied his father, "he has put an offering upon Athene's altar and has prayed for grace in the dance."

All night long the city was full of prayer and holy song and sacred dance. No god was forgotten. To every one was paid the thanks that was due him for yellow grain fields, or heavy vines, or thick-fleeced sheep, or plentiful rain, or warm sunshine, or good sailing winds, or health, or strength in the games.

One chorus sang:

"Come hither, Olympian gods, to our dance, and glorify it with your presence. In sacred Athens visit the city's hearth, where incense always burns, and visit her famous market-place. Accept our violet-twisted crowns, and drink offerings of spring-gathered herbs."

As the morning began to come, the songs and dances ceased. The groups thinned before the temples. People snatched hasty breakfasts. By the time the sun was up, all of Athens was deserted, except the broad street of the Ceramicus. Here all was laughter and shouting and pushing. Youths on restless horses, warriors in full armor, old men in spotless linen himations, women in soft colors, jostled one another in the middle of the street.

"Your horse is tramping on my himation," cried a dandy to a young warrior on horseback.

"Why is your himation in the street, then?" the warrior laughed back. "Is this a place for trailing robes?"

"A soldier's chlamys is in no danger of being trampled upon," called another young warrior teasingly.

"Do you not see that a himation is more becoming to our friend Aratus?" laughed some one else. "You will not find him in a soldier's cape if he can help it. Off with you, Aratus! See, there are the other women! Off with you!" and he pushed him with his spear, while the crowd laughed.

The porticoes at the side of the road were filled with men, old and young. A father was lifting up his little son.

ATHENIAN WARRIORS, WEARING CHITONS

"See," he said, pointing to a warrior, "there is the man who got the crown for bravery in our last battle. The arm that is under his chlamys has a deep wound."

"A victor! A victor!"

The shout was louder than all the noise of laughter and talk. A dozen young men were pushing people to right and left. They had a man on their shoulders and were running ahead of him, while he swayed and laughed above people's heads. Everybody turned to look, and then shouted his name.

Women and girls were crowded around the doors of the sacred storehouse, from which priests were bringing out platters and vases of gold. The priests put them into the hands of the waiting girls and women. Heralds were hurrying about among the crowd, shouting orders. The Panathenaic procession was forming.

On the porch of a little temple was standing a small group of men, less noisy than the rest.

"This festival is one of the best things in our country," one man said. "Here are fishermen from the seashore, timber-cutters from Hymettus, quarrymen from Pentelicus, shepherds from the mountains, grape-growers from the hills, farmers from the plains, poets and musicians from the streets of our city, guests from the colonies. All are talking together, finding out new things, making new friends. All are learning to call Athens 'mother.' "

Just then a herald came up to the men.

"We are ready for the officers of the city," he said. "Will you come, Pericles?"

The man who had been speaking stepped down from the porch. He turned to his friend.

"I will see you on the Acropolis, Phidias," he said.

In a little while the procession was ready. Flute-players and trumpeters were first. Behind them young men were leading the cattle for the sacrifice. There were a hundred animals, the fattest, the most beautiful, in all Attica. Their sleek sides shone with careful rubbing. Gold tips glistened on their horns. Garlands of flowers swayed from their slow-moving heads. And there were a hundred rams, with washed wool and hanging garlands.

Behind these animals walked the priests of Athens, in their long, old-fashioned robes, rich in color and glistening with gold embroidery. Wreaths of flowers crowned their heads, and garlands hung loose over their shoulders and arms.

ATHENE, FROM AN EARLY VASE-PAINTING

Then came people carrying the holy dishes, to serve Athene's feast on the Acropolis. There were women with baskets of bread and silver plates of cakes, young men with great black and red vases of wine, girls balancing on their heads baskets of flowers and fruit.

More than a thousand people followed with gifts for Athene,—little statues of terracotta, dishes of gold, bronze tripods, marble tablets with carved letters, gold-embroidered himations, necklaces of amethyst, carved golden bracelets set with coral.

And best of all the gifts was the great robe for Athene's statue. It hung as a sail in a beautiful ship. The boat rolled on hidden wheels, as though the wind itself carried it. The great yellow robe of soft wool waved gently. Athene and the giants in gold embroidery seemed to be moving in battle.

Behind the robe came the proudest men in Athens, the victors in the Panathenaic games. There was the best jumper, the best disc-thrower, the fastest runner, the best boxer, the best wrestler. The winner in the chariot-race rode in his chariot and reined in his nervous horses. There was the winner of the torch-race, with his torch still burning. The band of youths who had won the war-dance walked together, with swords in hand and helmets on their heads.

GREEK CHARIOT

The procession marched between rows of low houses. On the flat roofs stood people looking down. As the animals and their leaders and the bearers of gifts passed, the people on the house-tops waved their himations and threw down flowers; but when the victors came, the men shouted, and the women leaned over and showered them with blossoms.

"The victors, the victors!" they cried. And the victors looked up and smiled and caught at the flowers.

"There is the beauty of youth," men thought, as they looked at these victors. "But age, too, is beautiful. See those old men, with bodies well trained, still strong and straight. In their faces shine not youth, but wisdom and goodness."

For the handsomest old men of Athens had been chosen to walk behind the victors. They carried branches of Athene's olive.

Young warriors on prancing horses followed them. The wind lifted their bright capes and showed their shining armor beneath. After them came all the warriors of Athens,—some on horse, some on foot. Some carried fresh wounds from late battles. Again the shouts of the watchers rang loud.

"No wonder Athens has luck in battle," said one of the visitors. "See the number of her warriors, the richness of their armor!"

No freeman of Athens was willing to be left out on this great day.

"I will walk in Athene's procession, to do honor to my goddess and my city," every man said.

So, in their most beautiful himations, men walked quietly together, and their wives and daughters followed. Beside these women were others, carrying parasols and little stools. They were foreigners who had come to live in Athens.

"We are foreigners in the city," they said, "but we love it. We are willing on this day to make ourselves servants, if we may walk in the greatest and most beautiful procession of all Greece."

WOMEN OF ATHENS AT THE PANATHENAIC FESTIVAL

Not only the house-tops were filled with people looking on. In open places platforms had been built, and they were filled with gay men and women. People stood in the porches of temples, or crowded the corners of the market-place. They were visitors from all the world, come to see this great festival. Athenian women were there who could not take the long walk, and fathers and mothers who were too old to go, and children who were too young. Houses and columns and statues were hung with garlands of flowers. The city would not be so beautiful again for four years, until the next Panathenaic festival.

In the distance, all the time, ahead of the procession, the Acropolis arose. The great bronze Athene watched her people come. Her shining spear seemed to beckon them.

Now they had left the market-place and were winding up the steep front of the Acropolis. All foreigners had stayed behind. Only freemen of Athens might set foot on the Acropolis,—men and women with heroes for ancestors. They looked up lovingly at the tall bronze Athene. The people had had that statue made at the end of the Persian wars. They had found on the field of Marathon many bronze helmets and swords and spear-points of the Persians. They had gathered them together and had taken them to Athens and given them to Phidias, saying:

"Athene has helped us in this war. We wish to honor her. You are a great artist. Make us a statue of her from this bronze. We will put it upon the Acropolis. Then she can look over Athens. We shall live under her eyes. Give her a shield and a helmet and a spear, as though she were ready for battle. Make her tall, so that sailors in their ships can see her shining spear and helmet as they come into Athens; then they will know that the strong Athene guards our city."

Before the Persian war, temples and statues had covered the Acropolis. Now it was littered with broken stone and wooden storehouses. Rough rock altars stood up here and there. On this day they were bright with flowers.

The long procession walked past the bronze Athene and among the ruins, and stopped before a little temple. It was bare and unbeautiful. It had been put up in a hurry after the war. Here was the sacred olive tree. Here was Athene's holy statue, made of olive wood. It had dropped from the sky, men said, ages ago. It had gone on a ship to Salamis during the Persian wars. It was not beautiful, but it was the most precious thing in Athens, a gift from Athene's own hand. It was a post with a head carved on the top. The face was painted. Real hair hung from the head. A robe covered the post-shaped body. For hundreds of years Athenians had prayed at the altar before this statue, and it had grown dear to them.

GREEK HORSEMEN IN THE PANATHENAIC PROCESSION
From the Frieze of the Parthenon

Now the priestesses of Athene stood on the temple-porch to meet the procession. Maidens took down the beautiful robe from the ship and carried it to the priestesses, who took it into the temple. While the great crowd outside sang in praise of Athene, the priestesses took off the old robe and folded it and put it away in a treasure-chest. Then they put on the new one, clean and shining. And when it was done, they prayed to the goddess. Then they went out again and received the other gifts for Athene. They carried them in and piled them by the altar. It was a beautiful mass of precious things. After that they returned to the singing crowd, and all together marched on to the huge rock altar of Athene.

Then the umpires of the games stepped out before the people. One of them carried olive crowns in his arms. Others had baskets holding small black and red vases.

"Let Creon, the winner of the boys' footrace, approach," called one of the officers.

A slender lad stepped forward. He held his head high. The breath came quickly through his nostrils. The officer lifted a wreath and put it on the boy's head.

"I crown you Athene's victor," he said.

That whole great crowd shouted with joy.

"Creon, Creon! the Panathenaic victor!"

The officer gave Creon one of the vases. It was filled with olive oil. That oil was made from the fruit of Athene's holy olive tree.

The boy took the vase and stepped back among his friends. They clapped him on the shoulder and talked to him twenty at once. It was a great thing to be victor in the Panathenaic games.

Meanwhile the officers were calling up the other

victors. And as every one stepped back with his prizes, the happy crowd shouted.

After it was all over the priests walked to the altar. The men led up the animals of the sacrifice.

"Sing praises to Athene!
Give thanks to her for victory,
Give thanks for wisest counsel,
For skill with loom and spindle,
With sculptor's maul and chisel:
Give thanks for many blessings.
Sing praises to Athene!"

So sang the crowd; and while they sang, the priests killed the animals with their holy knives. The winner of the torch-race put his flame to the fuel on the altar. Soon the smoke of the sacrifice was rising to Athene, and the sweet smell of it was floating over the Acropolis. Then a herald stood by the altar and prayed,

"May the gods bless the Athenians and the Platæans."

After that all the people sat there by the altar and feasted,—a great family as Athene's guests. They talked of her goodness, of the wars of Athens, of the officers of the city, of new laws, of the games just over.

"Our great festival is finished," said a man to his neighbor. "I wonder what Athene will give us in the next four years to thank her for."

"The wisdom of Pericles will be one thing, I hope," replied his neighbor. "I believe he has great things in his mind for Athens. We never had so wise an officer in the city before, I think."

After the feast some people hurried home. Some went away together for gay banquets. Others were off for the gymnasium. A few stayed and strolled about on the Acropolis.

Pericles and Phidias walked slowly together.

"I am not willing, Phidias," said Pericles, "that this beautiful procession shall any longer end on a ruined hill. This Acropolis is the head of Athens. It should be beautiful, as she deserves. Our walls are done. Piræus is built. We are lords of the sea. We are rich, but we are not yet beautiful. Persian fire ate our temples and statues. It is time that we build them again. It is my dream to make Athens queen in loveliness. I wish her to be the shrine of beauty, where men shall come from all the world to fill their eyes and their souls.

PERICLES

"Years ago men started the work,—Themistocles and Cimon. See, there is the broad foundation where the temple of Athene was to rise. Here are the steps that were to lead up to it. The gods and the people need new temples. Let us get to work, Phidias."

"It is a glorious thing to do," said Phidias.

The two men stayed for a long time, looking at the ruins, measuring distances. At last, as they went down the hill, Pericles said:

"Talk with Ictinus to-morrow. He is, surely, the best architect in Greece. Make your plans, then get your artists together and begin the sculpture. I will send workmen to the quarries immediately."

Soon after that the Acropolis was busy with workmen. They were cleaning away the broken stones, measuring and marking lines on the rock platform. Stonecutters were chiseling blocks into shape. Drivers were urging their mules up the slope, dragging loads of marble.

Miles away, on Pentelicus, quarrymen were splitting out great pieces and sending them crashing down the slides. Stonecutters were smoothing and squaring them. And all along the road, from Pentelicus to Athens, were creaking carts loaded with marble.

Phidias' shop, too, was a busy place. As people passed it, they looked with glowing eyes at the bare walls.

"Behind that wall," they said, "the beauties of Athens are being made."

They watched the dozen men going in.

"There is a young sculptor from Argos," one said to another. "There is one from Ægina, and another from Thebes. Peace or war makes no difference to artists. They come from cities that hate us, because they love beauty and Phidias."

Then Phidias himself came around a corner. He was an old man, with bald head and stooping shoulders. He was staring far ahead.

"He is thinking of his statues," a watcher said to his friend, in a low voice. "They say that Athene sends him visions in dreams."

When Phidias went into the shop on this day, his pupils were already at work. Many young men had come from the cities of Greece to learn under him. Some few did good work. These he set to sculpturing a statue or a slab. The poorer workers he set to chiseling out the first rough shapes. Now there was a gay chatter and humming of songs as the mallets struck and the chips flew.

Clay models stood on tables, for the sculptors to work from. Phidias' charcoal sketches and paintings on wood lay about. The floor was white with marble dust. Corners were littered with broken pieces and cast-away statues left unfinished. The men were in short chitons. Clothes, hair and skin were dusty with marble.

Phidias stopped before a slab. A young man was working at it. He was sculpturing a woman carrying a basket. Phidias put his hand on the young man's shoulder.

"I am afraid it will not do, Alcestor," said he, in a kind voice. "It is stiff and awkward. There are too many folds in the robe. People will stop to count them. They will forget what it is all about. It is the same with the hair. Hair does not hang in such precise locks, does it? You work carefully. Your hand is skillful. But you must train your eyes to see what is beautiful. Look at this figure." He led him to another slab. "You think of what this woman is doing. You think of the procession in which she walks. You remember the goddess whom she is going to worship. You do not notice her hair or the folds of her robe. Let us try again."

So the unfinished slab was thrown into the corner. Phidias took off his long himation and stood in his short chiton. Then he set to work helping his pupil to start again.

After a while he went on to another piece of work. He stood before it, smiling, watching the sculptor. The young man was making his chisel fly, from foot to head, from waist to shoulder. He stepped quickly to and fro. He bent his head from side to side. Phidias laughed.

"You are a dashing artist, Charicles. You remind me of Phaethon, who tried to drive the sun's chariot. You must learn to drive first. Steady, steady! Do not make a stroke before you know what it will do. See!"

He took the artist's chisel and mallet and chipped delicately at the marble.

"The arm is well shaped, but it is rough. The muscles stand too high."

At first he talked as he worked, explaining. But soon he forgot everything except the statue. His pupil saw slowly grow under the master's tool a strong arm, where the muscles seemed almost to move. Some of the artists had gathered around to see Phidias work. At last he stopped and looked up at them, smiling.

"But I must go to my Athene," he said.

He gave back the tools and walked away to a quieter corner. Here stood a tall figure wrapped in damp cloths. These he carefully unwound. A helmet of yellow clay peeped out, then a strong face, a raised hand. And at last the whole figure was bare. The rough edges of the robe, the shapeless hand, the smeared lips, showed that it was still unfinished.

> "Quickly she leaped from the head
> Of the counselor Zeus,
> Shaking her spear and flashing her mail
> Till high Olympus trembled in dread
> And the wide earth shook below
> At the maiden's strength,
> And the dark sea boiled and broke in foam,"

chanted Pericles from the doorway.

Phidias turned quickly.

"Welcome, Pericles," he cried; "come in. It is a long time since you visited us. Yes, this is Athene."

"She is wonderful," said Pericles. "She moves. I can tell from her alone what is happening in the whole picture."

"But come," Phidias urged; "let me show you the rest of the work. Here is the Zeus that Alcamenes is chiseling. I shall put the finishing touches upon it in a few days. Here is the block of marble that is to make Iris. The stonecutter will begin to shape it to-morrow. This is the clay model. She is running to tell the world of Athene's birth. Three nights ago I dreamed how to make her. The gods are helping me, Pericles."

ZEUS

"And you are helping Greece," Pericles answered. "These pupils of yours will go back to their cities and fill them with beauty, as you are filling ours."

"I hope they will do something," said Phidias; "but they cannot do so much as I shall be able to do. They have no Pericles to put them to work. They can make beautiful statues, but they cannot make a whole beautiful city. That is the task you have set me. But come and talk while I work. I cannot answer, but I can listen."

So, while the artist walked about his figure, carving the lips with his tool, smoothing the cheeks with his thumb, shaping the hand, stepping back to look at his work, Pericles sat on a block of marble and talked.

"I can see this new Athens, Phidias," he said. "The temple of Athene and a new Erechtheum are glowing on the Acropolis. Gates, porches, steps, are shining on the slope. Another theater on the hillside rings with music. Beautiful halls surround the market-place. A temple honors every god.

"Themistocles saved Athens from the Persians. Themistocles and Cimon gave her walls and ships and power. We will give her beauty. That will be as great a service, I think. Our city wants good men. We will make them with beautiful statues, buildings, pictures. Perhaps the gods are good because they see nothing ugly in Olympus. Let us try it with men in Athens. Let them, when they pray, see statues, ceilings, walls, that remind them of Olympus. You have seen how happy people are when they are looking at a beautiful picture. Let us give them many such chances to be happy.

"And how people will love a city that shines with beauty! They will walk about happy, looking at temples and statues, and saying proudly to themselves: 'This is our city. She is worth the best we can give her,—honesty, kindness, bravery.'

"I stood to-day gazing at your bronze Athene. My heart grew strong. I said to myself: "My enemies, my worries, are only little things. I will keep on at my work and fear nothing.' Surely her brave lips have put courage into many men. Surely her calm eyes have soothed many angry hearts. We need more such statues."

Phidias turned from his modeling.

"And one of them must be in the new temple," he said. "But what shall it be? I am all in the dark. I have made many Athenes, but I am not satisfied. This one must be truer than any one yet. Athene has so many sides! She is the fierce goddess of war. She is the loving one who teaches me to work with my hands. She is the giver of health. She is the goddess of wise counsel. She is wonderful always, but how is she best? Which way will make her people love her most, will best please the savior, the lover of Athens? I cannot tell. Perhaps she will tell me in a dream."

The work on the Acropolis had been going on for seven years. Pericles was there watching one afternoon. Workmen were bringing up the pieces of sculpture for the metopes from Phidias' shop. Some were already there, and men were hoisting them into place. Others had been set, and scaffolds hung below them. Here artists were standing putting on the last touches of the chisel. Stonecutters were making the grooves in the tall columns. Others, at a little distance, were cutting joints on marble blocks. Pulleys and ropes were creaking. Mallets and chisels were pounding. Men were shouting orders.

Pericles found Phidias in a little wooden shop. Here it was more quiet, but just as busy. Goldsmiths, with little hammers, were beating out plates of gold. Ivory workers were sawing great tusks into strips, or were carving the thin pieces.

"And here you are making the beautiful Athene!" Pericles said.

Phidias looked up from the gold he was hammering.

"Yes," he answered. "Did you see the core for it in the temple? It is all finished."

"I saw it," laughed Pericles; "but I confess that it does not look to me much like a statue or anything else beautiful. I call it a tangle of wood and iron. But I will trust you to make it beautiful," he laughed again. "Every one here seems busy."

"I have not even had time," Phidias said, "to go down to the shop and find how things are there."

"I will go and see and report to you," said Pericles, and was off.

As he walked through the door of the shop, it seemed to him a different place from the one he had been used to see. There was little ringing of chisels and noise of moving blocks. In the corners and along the wall stood finished statues. Some were wrapped in great cloths, but some were uncovered. Artists were working on these, tinting the white marble with soft colors. One of the young men turned as he heard a footstep.

HEPHÆSTUS

"Ah, Pericles!" he cried; "you are in a glorified shop; Athene smiles at us," pointing to a marble statue. "Zeus, Apollo, Hephæstus, Poseidon," still pointing here and there at different statues. "We are among the gods."

"And you have lived among the gods for seven years," said Pericles.

The artist's gay smile vanished. Quickly his face flushed, and his eyes glowed.

"Yes," he said softly; "and it has been a blessed life. I have had these calm faces looking upon me day after day. I have seen what a man can do with marble.

I have seen Phidias dreaming, dreaming and making perfect beauty. I have felt my own hands grow skillful, and my eyes trained to see loveliness. I cannot tell which of these things has been best."

Another artist had come up to listen.

"It has been a wonderful time for us all," he said. "Oh, to do something worth doing! That is joy. I traveled for a little in Persia a few years ago. The idleness of it disgusted me. Themistocles did a good thing when he set you Athenians to work. And you have not forgotten your lesson. Work, work! You can feel it in the air of Athens."

"And we are not drudges, either," said the other artist, an Athenian. "We work because we like to work. I have seen men in Egypt building a temple. They were driven like slaves. They must have hated that building. We love every stone that goes into this temple."

"We must thank the gods that we are Greeks," said Pericles.

"And the pupils of Phidias," added the artist.

The sun was sinking below the mountains. The new temple cast a long shadow on the hilltop. Workmen were gathering up their tools. The Parthenon was finished. On the next day the festival of Athene would begin. Five days later the people of Athens would give this temple to the goddess and would worship there for the first time.

A group of workmen stood off, looking at the building.

THE ACROPOLIS, RESTORED

"I am proud to be a stonecutter," said one.

"Every stone, every joint, perfect!" said another. "It will stand for a thousand years."

"We have laughed at Ictinus for his fussy notions," another said, "but it was worth while. Those columns have wings; they seem so light. Oh, the trouble we had getting the curve right!"

"And the floor!" laughed a fourth man. "Ictinus would not have it flat. 'If it is flat, it will not look flat,' he said. He was so particular about the curve that my eye has learned to see a bump half a hair high."

"But no one will think of those things when he looks at the building," said the first man. "People will see the rich color, the shining columns, the shadowed porch, the lifelike statues. Oh, it is perfect!"

Again the Panathenaic procession wound up the front of the Acropolis. Every eye was big, every breath came quick. For years people had watched this temple grow,—glistening white walls, columns, roof. Then they had seen the dark blues and reds painted upon the flat spaces. The great statues were lifted up and set where they belonged. The carved slabs were put into place. Scaffolds had hung upon the building for artists and sculptors to work from. At last the scaffolds had been taken down. All this the people had seen daily as they worked in the city streets. But few had been close to the work. Guards at the gate had kept visitors away, but now they were to see everything.

THE FATES

As the procession reached the top of the hill and started along the flat ground, every eye was on the Parthenon. More slowly and more slowly people walked, looking. They had no words to say. The building floated before them more lovely than their dream. The deep, still porches, the dashes of warm color, the calm, white columns stretching away from them, the story in tinted marble,—all these things tied their tongues and drew their hearts out of them.

Here in the pediment were Athene and Poseidon striving for Athens. There stood their horses and chariots, large as life. Poseidon angrily turned to go. Athene joyfully strode to step into her chariot. And the pediment was crowded with her happy friends. All these statues shone with bronze and gold and color. Below were the great white columns and the shady porch. The wall at the back was brightened with painted and gilded vines and bands. The porch stretched down the long side and all around the building. Under its roof, at the top of the flat wall, the people saw in painted marble relief the very procession in which they were marching. It was going, as they were going, toward the east.

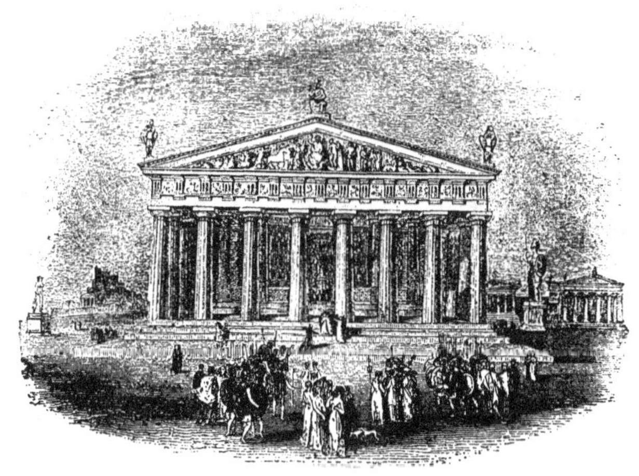

EAST END OF THE PARTHENON

All this they saw in the soft shadow of the morning sun. Then they turned the corner and saw the eastern end in a flood of golden sunshine. Every blue and red background in metope or pediment glowed. The gilded eaves, the golden ornaments on peak and on statues, burned. The level beams of the sun shot under the broad porch. They shone upon the gods seated there in marble relief above other columns, waiting to receive the procession. And in the pediment Athene had just sprung from the head of Zeus. "And the gods stood about and watched with awe."

The people could be silent no longer. They forgot the holy prayers to come. They shouted,

"Athene, Athene!"

And for a minute they turned to talk among themselves.

"I feel as though I were treading the meadow of Olympus and gazing at the gods themselves," said one.

"It seems like a living thing," spoke some one else.

After a moment of gazing, the procession began to march in through the great bronze doors. As soon as people passed the threshold, they fell silent. For there, far in the great, dim room, shone a statue. It was lit by one wide beam of sun. Tall as the room, Athene looked mildly down upon the hushed crowd. Her trailing robe, the helmet, the shield that rested at her feet, were all of gold, richly carved. The Victory that stood in her outstretched hand was of gold. Her face and neck, her arms, her feet that pushed out from under her robe, were of soft-tinted ivory. In the half-darkness she shone softly, as the real goddess might have done, if she had stepped down from Olympus. Looking into her calm

INTERIOR OF THE PARTHENON

face, people forgot their griefs and worries. Many men remembered the words of the old poem,

> "Pallas Athene does not permit me to tremble."

Then the room rang with a great song from the people of Athens:

> "Athene, we stand at thy feet,
> We lift our hands in prayer.
> Thy ears are filled with the prayers of the world,
> Thy nostrils breathe the smoke of a thousand shrines,
> And yet thou wilt not forget the town of thy name.
> Thou art wise; make us wise.
> Thou art brave; make us brave.
>
> "Oh! ward off war from our town
> And fill our walls with peace.
> Thy house shall be rich, Athene, with gifts;
> The walls shall be hung with picture and slab,
> The corners heaped with vases of gold,
> And incense burning above thy head,
> The columns hung with broidered cloth,
> The pavement piled with jars of wine,
> The dimness lit with shining gems,—
> All these we will bring in our love for thee.
> Come down, Athene, and live in thy house;
> Come down, Athene, and bless thy town."

SOCRATES

It was in Athens, after the Persian war. The street was only a crooked, dusty lane. The rows of houses were like walls lining the road. Along the street came a man. All at once he stopped, slapped his leg, and said:

"O ho! Sophroniscus has a boy!"

He had stopped in front of a poor, mud-plastered house. A little branch of olive hung on the door. As he stood there, a great knock came from the inside of the house. The man jumped away. Out swung the wooden door. It half blocked the narrow street. A man came out and shut it behind him.

"Good-morning, Sophroniscus. So you have a little son? Happy man!"

"Yes, a little son, Gylippus! I am going now to the temple of Here, to make her a thank-offering. So good-by! But you must come to the naming-feast." And off he ran down the street.

On the tenth day Gylippus did come, and many other friends. Sophroniscus was only a poor stonecutter. He had no servants to tend the door. His brother was opening it for visitors on this day. The guests walked into the little open court and stood chatting there. After a time, Sophroniscus came out to them.

"Good-day, my friends; I am glad to see you. Come in and be seated. I have no grand house nor entertainment to offer you."

"That's a gay himation you have in honor of the new baby. The red border!" said a friend, smiling.

"Oh, even a poor man must have a new himation at the naming-feast. But you shall see the baby."

He went into another room and came back carrying a wee baby. It was a stiff little bundle. A narrow cloth was wrapped around and around, from feet to neck.

"What big eyes he has," said a woman.

"He has a lusty voice; he will be an orator," Gylippus said.

Everybody had something to say about the baby.

"Now, friends," said Sophroniscus, "if you will come to the altar, I will give him his name."

They walked to one corner of the court. A little wooden altar, with a clay statue of Zeus, stood there. Some of the guests had brought gifts. They placed them on the altar, to ask Zeus to be kind to the boy. Sophroniscus, holding the baby in his arms, walked three times around the altar. He stopped before it and prayed, saying:

"O Father Zeus, here is my little son; I will call him Socrates. Do thou be kind to him."

Then they all went into the room again and had a feast and talked of the little Socrates, promising that he should be a great sculptor or a great athlete or a great orator. But he grew up to be a greater man than they dreamed of.

The little Socrates had not much care as he grew up. His father was away all day at his shop, and his mother was often out; for she was a nurse. When he was five or six years old, he was often left alone. The door was shut, and he played in the house and the court until his father and mother came home at night. So his little chiton was often dirty, and his hair tangled. But he was a healthy, happy boy. He rolled his hoop about the court, or played knucklebones. His father had brought him little blocks of stone from the shop. He would build houses with them, or even chip at them, playing stonecutter. Sometimes he went with his father to the shop. There he played with the tools and wished that he could be a real stonecutter. Sometimes he went across the street to a sandal-maker's shop. Hippias, the sandal-maker, liked him. He said once:

"O Socrates, you ask more questions than a woman. You surely will be a philosopher when you grow up."

Soon after he was seven years old, Sophroniscus took him on his knee one night. He smoothed his rough hair lovingly.

"Socrates, you are seven years old now. When

rich men's sons are as old as that, they begin to go to school. I haven't much money to spare, but I want my boy to be educated. When you become a man, you will go to the public assembly and vote for the laws. You will be president of the assembly some time, too. I want you to be a good citizen and a good president, and an ignorant man can't be that; so I have made arrangements for you to begin school to-morrow."

"Oh, good! Oh, I'm glad, father! I'm going to school! Mother, mother, I'm going to school!" And off he ran to the hearth, where his mother was cooking.

Soon he was back.

"Then I must get up early in the morning, mustn't I?"

"Indeed you must; school begins at sunrise."

The next morning, in the gray, early light, Sophroniscus and Socrates were standing on a street-corner near their house. Socrates had a little basket in his hand. He was dancing around his father and laughing and talking about school.

"When will they come, father? The sun will be up in a little while. Oh, here they are, here they are!"

Down the street came marching a line of boys. Almost every boy was walking beside a man and holding his hand. The man carried a basket or a little bundle of tablets and books. Socrates took his father's hand and smiled up at him.

"You are my pedagogue, father. You are better than any servant."

INTERIOR OF A GREEK SCHOOL

"Yes, and here we go." And they fell in at the end of the line.

As the column turned in at the school-house door, Socrates left his father, saying:

"Good-by, father, I'll tell you all about it to-night."

The building where they were turning in was a one-story white-plastered house. When they came into the court, Socrates turned to the boy behind him and said:

"E-h-h! Pretty!" His eyes were shining.

The court was a large one. It was filled with oleanders, palms and rosebushes. Around the sides, in front of the room-doors, were covered walks. Columns, painted rose-color and white, held up the roof. In front of Socrates stood a marble statue of Athene. Her robes were purple; her shield and spear were gilded.

A grave-looking man came into the court from one of the rooms.

"Good-morning, boys. You are well again, Alcmenor? I see you have a new chlamys, Pheido. And this is Socrates, our new boy? I am glad to see you, Socrates."

BOYS WITH LYRE

He put his hand on the boy's shoulder.

"But now it is time for lessons," he called out to them all.

They went trooping into different rooms.

Oh, that was a great day for Socrates! Everything was new and beautiful. He went into a room with several other little boys. They sat on long stone benches around the sides of the room. On the wall hung lyres and tibas. A young man sat on a chair in the front. He had a lyre on his knee.

"Take your lyres," said the teacher.

Each boy took a lyre from the wall. The plectrum hung from it by a ribbon. Socrates had never held a lyre before, but he had often seen other people play them. So he set it on his knee and put his left hand behind it, and took the plectrum in his right hand, just as he ought to do. The teacher looked at Socrates and said:

"What is the new boy's name?"

"Socrates."

"Do you wish to learn to play the lyre, Socrates?"

"Yes."

"Why?"

"Because it is beautiful."

"Socrates, I wish you to study music, because it will make you graceful and gentle. A man who knows nothing of music will be cruel and ungentlemanly. Now tune the strings." And so the music-lesson went on.

After a while the boys went into another room. There another master taught them how to make letters on wax tablets.

"This is not so much fun as the music," thought Socrates.

He heard the bigger boys in the next room. They were reciting poetry.

"Some time I shall be able to do that," thought he, "and that will be fine."

Late in the morning his class went into still another room. There they began to learn to count. At the end of that lesson school was over for the morning. Everybody ran laughing and shouting into the court. The pedagogues of the rich boys brought lunches and spread them out for their little masters. Socrates had only some slices of bread spread with honey. He had soon finished eating and was talking to Cleon, a boy near him.

"Was it you reciting poetry this morning?"

"Yes; and I got my knuckles cracked because I didn't stand gracefully."

"Oh, do you stand when you say it?"

"Why, yes, boy. Don't orators stand when they speak? And aren't we all trying to be orators? And mustn't orators be graceful?"

HOMER

"But you weren't making a speech."

"No, of course not. I'm not old enough nor wise enough yet. You have to know all of Homer and be able to chant it and play it before you can be an orator. But come on; there's the gong. We must go to the gymnasium."

All the boys jumped up and formed in line again. They marched out and down the street a little way and into a small gymnasium. All the pedagogues stopped at the door and waited on the outside. Socrates had often seen the outside of a gymnasium before, but never had been inside. He had dreamed about the fine games in there and had wished that he might peep in. But now he was really going to play there. While he was looking around in wonder, a man touched him sharply with a stick.

"Off with your clothes," he said.

Socrates ran into a dressing-room. He was back in a minute.

"Throw this ball to Cleon," said the master, and gave him a ball.

Little Socrates could not throw very well and was soon tired. But every minute or two the master was there and would say:

"Throw it harder; run for it; put your hands closer together."

When Socrates thought his arms would drop off with the ache, the master said:

"Come here with these boys and jump."

It gave his arms time to rest. After the jumping, came work with the dumb-bells. Then the master had him run around and around the gymnasium court. He showed him how to swing his arms and how to lift his feet high. The sun was just going down when he said:

"That's all. Take your bath and go home."

The boy ran to a great vase in the court. He threw water upon himself and rubbed it off with his hands. Then he rubbed his body with olive oil. He felt his muscles grow limber under it. At last he scraped himself with his strigil. He put on his chiton, and hung his strigil and oil vase at his girdle. He put a fresh fillet on his hair.

When he came out of the gymnasium, there was his father.

"O father! I am glad you are here."

"Well, how did you like it, my boy?"

"Oh, it was fun! But I'm so tired!" And he leaned against his father.

"Well, come on home; you shall go to bed. In a few days it won't tire you so. What did you do?"

"O father! wait till I am rested."

Sophroniscus laughed.

"All right, my man. It is good for you, even if it does tire you. It will make you strong and healthy and handsome and able to work for Athens. A man with stiff hands and legs will have a stiff tongue, too."

And so Socrates lived for seven years,—school and gymnasium all day long; early to bed and early to rise. When he left school, the master said to him:

"You do not play the lyre very well, but you can recite all of Homer after a fashion. You know how to use numbers, and you are always asking questions. You will find out a great many things for yourself."

The master of the gymnasium said to him:

"You were born ugly, but you are one of the strongest and toughest boys in the gymnasium."

Socrates had left school early. He was to go to his father's shop and learn his trade. He worked away for several years. One day his father said to him:

"You are not a bad stonecutter, but you don't do much work. You wander about the streets, talking to people. You listen to the wise men. Here at your work I often find you drawing figures in the dust. Why don't you stop this nonsense and go to work?"

"I am trying to find what the sun is made of. I am wondering how the stars were made. I get to thinking about these things and forget to work."

"A poor man has no business to bother about the sun or stars," growled his father.

But Socrates earned enough to support himself. After a while he married and had a house of his own. He had a great many friends. His wife once said,

"You are always bringing your friends here, when we have nothing to eat."

"Ah, my dear, we feast on wise words."

And so they did. One of his friends once said,

"I should rather talk with Socrates than eat a fine dinner."

This same friend once went to the oracle at Delphi. Here Apollo had a temple and a priestess. Apollo knew all things and he was glad to help men with his wisdom. So people used to go to his temple to ask him questions through his priestess. And through this priestess he answered them.

Socrates' friend said to the priestess:

CONSULTING THE ORACLE AT DELPHI

"Is there any one wiser than Socrates?"

The priestess answered,

"No."

The friend was delighted. He thought to himself,

"How proud Socrates will be when he hears it."

He hurried back to Athens. He burst through the doorway of Socrates' house, calling,

"Socrates! the oracle says that you are the wisest man in the world."

Socrates turned and looked at him in wonder.

"What do you say, Chærephon?"

"The oracle says that you are the wisest man in the world."

"I wise?"

"Yes, you; and I think so, too."

"But I am not wise. What does the oracle mean? The oracle always tells the truth. But how can this be true? Is there nobody wiser than I am? Surely. But the oracle says not. I must find out. There are the officers of the city; they must be wiser. I will go and see whether they are not."

The next day he went to the chief of the city.

"You know how to rule the city, do you not?" asked Socrates.

"Oh, yes!" answered the chief.

"What kind of men ought to be officers?"

"Wise men."

"But what are wise men?"

"Why, men who know a great many things."

"What kind of things?"

"The things we learn in school,—music and numbers and gymnastics."

"Is that all?"

"Why-y, no; they must be orators."

"Why?"

"O Socrates, you are trying to make a fool of me!"

"No, indeed. I wish to know why an officer of the city ought to be an orator."

"In order that he may make the people do as he pleases."

"But what should he please to have them do?"

"Why, different things."

"Dance and turn somersaults?"

Some of Socrates' friends were there. When he said this, they laughed at the officer. This made the officer angry, and he said,

"I'll not talk to you; you are making fun of me."

And he always hated Socrates after that.

Socrates said to his friends as they left the building:

"I think that an officer ought to be a man who loves his city. He ought to know how to make men good and honest. I expected this man to be wise, but you see that he is not. Let us go to Meno, the maker of lyres. Surely he will be wise, since he makes such fine things."

So they went to Meno, and Socrates said,

"Meno, I hear that you make the finest lyres in Athens."

APOLLO, WITH LYRE

"I think it is true," said Meno.

"I suppose it is difficult to make a good lyre."

"Yes, a lyre-maker must know a great many things."

"Should you call a maker of lyres a wise man, then?"

"I should think so."

"Then I ask you, Meno, you wise man, do you know what a good man is?"

"Why, yes; a good man is a man who does nobody any harm."

"Then a dead man is a good man."

Socrates' friends laughed, and Meno flushed with anger.

"No. Well, then, a good man is one who does people good."

"But what is it to do people good?"

"Oh, you ask too many questions. I haven't time to bother with you."

Socrates turned to his friends.

"I begin to see what the oracle means. These men think that they know things when they don't know them. Now, when I don't know a thing, I say so. For instance, if you said to me, 'How many grains of sand are there in a cupful?' I would say, 'I don't know.' But these men would say, 'Five million,' or some such number. I think that is what Apollo calls being wise. But I will not be sure yet; I will try everybody. Perhaps I may teach people to be wise in this way."

So he went about to everybody. He talked with people on the street-corners. He talked with people in their shops. He talked with people who were buying in the market-place. He talked with the young men who lounged in the barber-shops. He always found the same thing,—people pretended to know things that they did not know. He tried to show these people that they were not wise. After that they always hated him.

SOCRATES

But it was wonderful the way his friends loved him. He was always being asked to banquets. Many rich men asked him to be teacher for their sons. They offered him a great deal of money to do it, but he always answered:

"No, I am not wise enough to be a teacher; I am only trying to make men good and honest. Of course I can't take money for that, because I am doing it for Apollo."

But there were some people who were very angry because their sons followed Socrates. They said:

"We never know where our sons are; we can't keep them at home or at school. This Socrates charms them like a siren."

One of the young men who loved Socrates was named Alcibiades. He was a very handsome fellow, and a sort of a dandy. It was strange to see these two walking together. Alcibiades had on a gay new himation every day; his hair was curled and perfumed. Socrates wore the same old gray robe winter and summer. He was usually barefooted; he was partly bald, and his gray hair was ragged. But Alcibiades said:

"Socrates is like a pigskin wine bottle. How ugly on the outside! But oh, the sweetness and sparkle when it is opened!"

One time the army of Athens marched away north to war. Alcibiades and Socrates were two of the soldiers. It was cold up there. The snow was deep. The soldiers seldom stirred out of camp. When they did go, they wore several cloaks and wrapped their feet in skins and felt. But Socrates still went barefooted and wore his one old himation.

One morning, when the summer had come, the soldiers saw him standing in front of the camp. He was staring at the ground in deep thought.

"What do you suppose he is thinking about?" asked the soldiers among themselves.

After an hour or two they looked again. He was still standing in the same position. They laughed and said,

"Let us watch him."

He did not move all day. At supper some of the soldiers said,

"Why not take our blankets out there and see whether he stays all night?"

So they did. They laughed and joked about him until nearly midnight. They then fell asleep. When they awoke in the morning, there he was still, thinking as deeply as ever. An hour or so after the sun rose he raised his head, clapped his hands, and said,

"Oh! now I see."

YOUNG ATHENIAN SOLDIERS

Then he prayed to Apollo and walked away.

"Did you ever think as hard as that?" asked one soldier of another.

"No, indeed."

"What do you suppose he was thinking about?"

"Oh, I don't know. Some hard thing."

In one battle Alcibiades and Socrates were in the same rank. Alcibiades was fighting fiercely with one of the enemy. Finally the man turned and ran back into his own lines. Alcibiades ground his teeth and shouted,

"I'll have you yet."

He did not think of the danger, but ran after him. In a minute he was surrounded by the enemy. A rough soldier raised his spear and said,

"Now, young dandy, say good-by to the sun!" and he threw his spear.

It pierced Alcibiades' leg. As he fell, he cried,

"Help! Socrates!"

Socrates heard and ran to the place. Another soldier had his sword raised, ready to kill Alcibiades.

"Ho there, you villain!" cried Socrates, and threw his spear.

Down fell the soldier. Socrates jumped and stood over Alcibiades. He held his shield low and caught a blow that was meant for Alcibiades. He answered with a sword-thrust. So he fought until the rest of the army came and saved them.

Some wicked men once made themselves officers

of Athens. They knew that they had no right to do it, and they said to themselves:

"A great many people hate us because we have done this thing. They will try to drive us out. We will kill all our enemies. Then we shall be safe."

There was a certain enemy of theirs, named Leon. He lived several miles away. They said,

"Let us send some other of our enemies after him. They are so afraid of us that they will bring him. Then they will be to blame for his death, and they will not dare to call us wicked any more."

So they sent for five men. One of the five was Socrates. When they came into the building, the officers scowled at them and said,

"Go and bring Leon to us."

The five men came out of the door. Their faces were pale, all but Socrates'. The four started off. They looked around for Socrates.

"Are you not coming?" they asked.

"Of course not."

"But they will kill you."

"It is better to die than to do a wicked thing."

The four shuddered when he said "die."

"Oh, we can't do that," they said.

So on they went and brought Leon, as they were told to do. But Socrates went home about his own business. When his wife heard of it, she cried and said,

"O Socrates! they will kill you."

"But you would not have me do a shameful thing?"

But these officers had no time to harm any one else. They were soon driven out of Athens.

Socrates was now an old man—seventy years old. But he was as strong as ever. He still went about the streets talking to everybody. The young men still loved him and followed him about. But he had a great many enemies. These enemies were always talking among themselves about Socrates. They did not know exactly what to say about him, for they could not say,

"I hate him because he proved that I was foolish."

So they said all sorts of things:

"He does not believe in the gods. He teaches our sons bad things and wastes their time."

And one man said:

"He taught my boy to make fun of me, his father, because I am a tanner."

Now the real story was this: Anytus, a tanner, had a very bright young son. Socrates one day said to him:

"You are a bright young fellow. You can do something besides tan leather; be an orator."

So these people kept talking among themselves and making themselves all the more angry. At last three men wrote out a charge and hung it up where everybody could see it, and had Socrates arrested. In a few days he must come to the court and be tried. His friends were frightened. They said:

"Get a great lawyer. Have him write your speech. Get men to speak for you. We will give you all our money, if you will only use it."

But Socrates only laughed.

"Why, I have been getting my speech ready all my life," he said.

"What do you mean?" they asked.

"I have been living honestly all my life. Is not that the best way to defend myself?"

At last the day came for the trial. The room was crowded with people. Socrates' friends stood with him before the jury. One of the men who had had him arrested stood up and said:

"Socrates does not believe in the gods; he teaches our sons bad things. I say that he ought to be killed."

Then he sat down, and it was Socrates' turn to speak. As he stood up, he smiled at the people.

"My enemies say that I do not believe in the gods, but listen: I have spent all my life trying to explain to the people what the oracle meant. I said, 'This is what Apollo means: the wise man is the one who knows that goodness is better than riches or glory.' So I went about trying to make people understand. When I found a man lying in order to get rich, I said, 'Are you not ashamed to love money better than truth?' When I saw a man angry at his brother, I said: "Do you not know that you ought to love your brother? You ought to do everything to make him happy.'

"My friends, you have seen a gadfly on a horse. The horse pokes along, with his head down, his ears lopped, half asleep, until the fly alights on him and bites him. Then he wakes up and trots. Well, you Athenians are the horses, and I am the gadfly. If I find you asleep when you ought to be working, I bite you and set you to work. If I see you going to eat a poison-weed, I bite you and drive you away. You ought to love me for that. But you are like lazy children, who don't like to be waked in the morning; so you say, 'Let us kill this gadfly,' and you hit at me.

"You say that I teach your boys bad things. I try to teach them to be honest and to love their city. Are these wicked things?

"You are saying to yourselves, 'Why doesn't he bring his wife and children here? If they fell on their knees before us and cried and said, "Who will take care of us if you kill Socrates?" we might let him off. Other men always do that; why doesn't he?' I will tell you why: I don't want you to let me go for pity. If you think I am wicked and ought to die, I want you to say so. I think it would be cheating if I made you sorry for me, and so coaxed you to do what you think to be wrong. If you think that you are doing right to kill me, I am willing to die. I am not afraid to die; all that I am afraid of is to do a wicked thing."

Then he sat down. The people who were standing in the courtroom whispered and scowled among themselves. The jury went out and voted. They came back, and one of them said:

"We think that Socrates is guilty; two hundred and eighty-one against him, two hundred and twenty for him."

Then the jury sat, waiting. Socrates had a right to make another speech. The man who had had him arrested had said,

"We think that he ought to die."

But Socrates now had a chance to say:

"I do not want to die, but I will suffer some other punishment; I will pay a fine. Will you take it and let me go?"

The men of the jury were thinking:

"He will offer to pay a great sum of money or to leave Athens. We will agree to that; he need not die."

Socrates rose to speak again:

"Well, you want me to offer some punishment for myself. What shall it be? Something that I deserve, of course. Now I say that I have been the best friend of Athens. When a man wins a foot-race, you feed him at the public building for thanks. I say that I have done you more good than I could by winning a foot-race, so

I say, 'Feed me at the public building with your other great men.'

"Do you want me to say that I will leave Athens? Think of me, an old man, trying to live in some new place. I was never in my life in any other city. I know the streets and buildings of Athens as I know my own fingers. I can walk blindfolded through the city; I love it as I love my mother. I would not live in any other place; I should always be wishing for Athens. No, I cannot leave Athens.

"Do you want me to pay a fine? But I am a poor man; I have only enough money to buy bread and clothes."

When he said that, three or four of his friends leaned toward him.

"Socrates, you may have all of our money. We are rich men; take all we have and buy yourself off," they said.

Socrates smiled and said to the jury:

"My friends offer me their money to use; but if I should pay a fine, it would be the same as saying, 'Yes, I am guilty.' But I am not guilty, so I will not pay a fine; neither will I leave Athens. But I will consent to be fed at the public building with the heroes. What will you do with me?"

Then he sat down. The jury scowled at him more than ever. They sneered and said:

"He thinks that it is a good joke about being fed

with the heroes. We will show him what we think of him."

So they voted again and said:

"We think he ought to die."

That was really the end of it; but Socrates arose again and said:

"May I talk to you a little while? The officers have not yet come to take me away. Do you think that you have done me any harm? You have not. I am glad, thinking of what will happen to me. When I die, I shall go to another country. There everybody is happy and kind. I shall see all the good men that ever lived. I can talk with them as long as I please. I can sit and chat with Achilles and Odysseus and Homer and Leonidas. I can ask them all about that great war at Troy, and the fight with the Persians. Ah, I shall be happy there. But here are the officers; I must go. Good-by, my friends!"

He came down the steps of the building. A young man who loved him came to him weeping.

"O Socrates!" he said, "it makes me weep to see you die and not deserve it."

Socrates put his hand on the young man's head and smiled.

"Should you rather have me deserve to die? You are a funny fellow."

So Socrates went to his prison. He was there about a month. Every day his friends came to talk with him. He was as kind and as happy as ever. One morning his old friend, Crito, came before sunrise and found Socrates asleep. He sat by the bed for a long time. At last Socrates awoke.

"Why, Crito! You here so early? How long have you been here?"

"An hour or so."

"Why didn't you wake me?"

"I have been watching you. You looked so happy in your sleep that I didn't want to wake you. I have bad news to tell."

"Oh, you mean that I must die to-day?"

"Yes, or to-morrow."

"Why, Crito, this is not bad news."

"Not bad for you, but for your friends. Socrates, I have given money to the doorkeeper of the prison. He will let you go away. Won't you go, Socrates?"

"Run away like a thief, Crito? And, besides, where could I go?"

"I have rich friends in Thrace. They have asked you to live with them. You could live like a king."

"But I don't want to live like a king, and I don't want to live anywhere but in Athens. But do you think it would be right for me to go, Crito?"

"Of course I do."

"But Crito, suppose the Laws should come to me and say: 'What are you doing, Socrates? Do you remember when you were eighteen years old? You came before all the men of Athens and said: "I promise always to obey the laws." You didn't have to promise that. You might have said: "I don't like Athens or its laws; I will go to some other city." But you did not say that. You said: "I love Athens; I love her laws; I will obey them; I am their son."' Didn't I say that, Crito?"

"Yes."

"Ought I not to keep my promise?"

"I suppose so."

"Then, besides, the Laws would say to me, 'Ought not a son to obey his father?' 'Yes,' I would say. 'Always?' they would ask. 'Yes, always.' 'But we, the Laws, are your father. Ought you not, then, to obey us?' Shouldn't I have to say yes, Crito?"

"I am afraid so."

"Perhaps the Laws would say this, too, 'Have you ever been in the army?' I should say: 'Yes!' 'Did you obey your captains?' 'Yes.' 'Always?' 'Yes.' 'Even when he said, "Go fight, and die if it is necessary?" ' 'Yes.' 'Suppose you had run away before the battle. What would men have called you?' 'A coward.' 'But we, the Laws, are your captain. Now we say, "Die." What ought you to do?' What do you say, Crito? Ought I to obey, then, and not run away?"

"I am afraid so, Socrates."

"Well, then, come, cheer up! Let us do our duty." And Socrates smiled at Crito.

On the next morning all Socrates' best friends

came to the prison. They came as soon as the doors were open. They talked all day long. Toward evening Socrates said,

"Well, bring in the poison."

They brought it, and he drank it. The last thing he said was:

"Crito, we owe a cock to Æsculapius; pay it, therefore, and do not neglect it."

Æsculapius was the god of healing. Whenever a Greek was cured of a sickness, he knew that Æsculapius had done it, and he took a thank-offering to his temple. Now Socrates expected death to cure him of ignorance and of wickedness. In the land of the dead he would learn much, and he would be happy. So he wished to thank the god of healing as other men did. His last words were really the Greek way of saying,

ÆSCULAPIUS

"Oh! I shall be very happy talking with Achilles and Leonidas and the others."

www.ingramcontent.com/pod-product-compliance
Lightning Source LLC
LaVergne TN
LVHW090949080826
845145LV00003B/948
9781599152707